To Stuart

you d[...]

you

A CHANCE TO ESCAPE

This is the story of
Alexa Ferilli

Written by
Vanessa Nocera

Table of Contents

1. It All Started in 2003...

I remember waking up in the middle of the night.

I was startled to hear my parents' voices, raised in the other room. I opened the bedroom door and crept down the hall to the bathroom.

My parents were arguing about a short business trip that my dad was planning to take—he wanted to save our flat from being repossessed and put up for sale at auction. Dad was always struggling with investments, and he had some businesses in Addis Ababa and Ethiopia. He had decided to go away for four days, although my mum was far from happy about the trip.

He was a good-looking man, my dad: six feet tall, with brown hair and green eyes. He was a wise man, always very polite, and everyone fell in love with his charming attitude. He was passionate about making money, and he could start up a dream business in a very short amount of time.

My dad was smart, and quick to seal a deal. He was that kind of guy who was good at selling—some might say good at talking, but I think the right word is "lying." He would lie about everything, especially while he was working. A mixture of a lawyer and a criminal, he showed the care of a president to his clients. A very good guy: that was how they all described him. He was involved in a very important fashion business, selling clothes around Italy; at least, that was what my mom and I were led to believe. But he was in debt with the government, and had never paid a bill in his life. He drove a white Ferrari, but it was bought in my mother's name.

He did not share a lot with us about his business, but he was a good father to me, and was always there whenever I needed him. For instance, he was the only one who knew when I first got my period. Although he promised me that was our little secret, he spread the news around the whole family. The day after, he organized a party, just for me.

My dad had two shops in the city's center, and whenever I was there, he was busy with cash flow, invoices, payrolls, and delivery. I remember a couple of times seeing two guys there asking for money, which he refused to give. The men were dressed in a stylish and composed manner, but they were imposing and a little threatening; the way they spoke to him, it was as if they were ready to push him to his limit and beyond.

The last time he met with them, I put my hands into his desk drawer, but to my horror I found that the gun he kept was no longer there.

The day of my dad's departure came, and I had stopped thinking about the men and my mom's displeasure at the trip; I was too excited at the prospect of spending the weekend with Dad to go fishing together upon his return. It was January 13, 2003. I was standing by my high school at 7:55 am. It was raining; my dad was kneeling. He held my hand and kissed my little fingers. Tears were in his eyes.

"Have a good day at school, Lexi! Your dad loves you—never forget that, please." He hugged me so tight that day. But I was only a teenager, and I didn't pay that much attention to those words.

I reached the last step of the stairway, and my heart stopped for a moment. I hesitated: I had this feeling that he was running away from me. But I needed to get to class, so I shook it off as just a bad feeling and kept walking down the corridor.

That Monday morning was the last time I saw my dad.

* * *

Late on Friday evening, it was raining once again. Raindrops crashed against the window. The house was empty. My mom was setting the table for three.

I stopped, and said, "Mum, when is Dad coming back? Is it today?"

She gazed at me. "Yes, honey, it is tonight, but I'm not sure what time. Now come, the food is getting cold."

Pasta was ready on the plates. We started eating and watched the news.

When we had dinner with Dad, it was fun and lively; he was always talking about something or other. We'd never had a quiet dinner before. But Mom was much too quiet that night.

My mother was a pianist; she dedicated much of her life to studying music. We had a piano in the living room, and whenever the cat walked across it, we could hear the notes from our bedrooms—being woken by disjointed piano sounds in the dark night hours is most unpleasant. Then I'd realize that it was him and go back to bed. Ambrogio was a large, grey cat with green eyes and white fur on his stomach and around his cheeks; other than my mother, he was the only one in the house to "play" the piano. Mom tried to push me to do so, but I was not really interested in learning.

Mom had given up her dream job to help dad with the business. I was 13 years old at that time, experiencing all the new things that a teenager discovers, such as their first kiss or first cigarette; I used to write it all in my diary, which I made sure was locked, and I had the only key.

With my dad though, it didn't matter: he knew everything about me. He was the only person that I ever felt truly comfortable talking to; he gave me good advice, and never let me down.

And so that night, it left me wondering: why has he left us? Why is he not back yet? Maybe he was running away from something—or someone?

It had been a week since he'd walked away from me at my high school that Monday morning. Mom had called the police. The whole family was in the living room, talking about my dad being missing. The cops arrived and started asking my mum if anything unusual had happened recently, or if she had seen anyone suspicious hanging around his business in the last week; she was aware of his short business trip, but nothing more than that.

They also asked me if he had been acting any different with me during the last week; if he had behaved strangely or said anything odd.

I didn't want to tell them about the gun having disappeared from his drawer. So, I just looked at the policeman in the eyes with a worried face and said, "No. I'm afraid, but I haven't noticed anything strange during the last week."

"Okay, fine. But if you do remember something, please call us."

"Sure, I will," I answered.

I would have told the truth if the cops had been genuine, but I didn't like the way they looked at my mom; they made me feel uneasy. I had a feeling that Dad was in trouble; I remembered those guys walking with him outside the shop, trying to ask for money.

I wasn't sure I needed to say this to Mom, so I decided to keep it to myself.

* * *

It had been two weeks since my dad left. I heard my mom crying in the middle of the night; she was waiting for me to fall asleep, unaware that I, too, could not sleep. I felt so helpless in our situation; it was hard to ignore my dad's unexplained absence, and I didn't know if I could handle it.

Looking at the stars of my bedroom wall, I couldn't help but think of him. Dad had bought me those phosphorescent stars that you can stick to the wall, so that when the light was off, it was like seeing bright stars in the night sky. It made me feel like I was in an open space.

I tried to have a silent cry, so I decided to push the pillow over my neck, then pushed it with my palms against my head. I spent all the night crying, so that the next morning my eyes were red and swollen.

In the morning, I got ready to go to school. For the first time I would be walking to school, as Dad always dropped me off in his car. I looked for him in the streets, by the entrance of the shops, at the school; I always checked every corner to see where he could be.

I had to remind myself that I was awake; that this was not just a dream that will soon end. Like a nightmare that vanishes once you open your eyes; but this was not a nightmare, it was not a dream … it was unwelcome reality.

The day was windy, and the birds welcomed me by the steps of my high school. The road was empty, empty like my heart now: like an exquisite vase without flowers, like the sky without stars, like a wedding without the bride. I felt like an empty shell: a cold sensation had frozen my mind, crushing my soul.

I stopped by the last step before the entrance. I was locked in that space for a moment, as if I were divided from the world: far away from people, far away from the noise of the students, far away from the chatter of the parents; as if I had stopped the clock to meditate for a moment.

That moment was my worst enemy; it didn't give me any notice when it came. It just came and destroyed my day, taking with it my ability to speak, making me a loser in the eyes of my peers, and keeping my concentration far away when I tried to study. In the days that followed I tried to control it, but what pitted itself against me was a strong, negative energy, an enemy too big for me to handle; in the end, I had to accept that it was the biggest enemy in the world.

I decided to give that enemy—my depression—a name: its name was Black Moon.

Everyone at school was aware that my dad missing. My teacher suggested talking with a child therapist, but that was not enough for me to discover the truth. I tried learning how to be calm and keep myself in a positive mood. I joined the after school program just to keep myself busy. This was not a good idea in the end, because I could then watch all the other dads waiting by the entrance to pick up their kids; it always made me think about my dad.

I decided to join the gym. In the middle of a class, a song started playing: it was the very song my dad had often sung to me. I could not hold back the tears.

The teacher told me to take a break. In the changing room, I imagined my dad was there talking with me; then, reality set in again: it was just me and my empty soul, crying alone on the toilet of the gym changing room.

Losing myself in the middle of the street one day, I saw the church at the end of the road. I walked in and started to cry. For me, there was no time for happy moments; I only knew I must let the feeling out.

Looking at Mary by the altar I prayed, asking where my dad could be. I prayed for a call, just one phone call, so I could hear his voice and feel better. A priest walked up to me; he smiled and asked me if I needed a confession.

"I don't know anymore," I said. "But if it helps my dad to come back, then maybe."

"Hold my hand," he said. "Tell me what's wrong and what happened; you shouldn't be alone when in church."

"My father is missing," I told him, "and I am unable to continue with my life; I feel empty and aimless."

He paused for a minute, gazing at me. "Pray for strength to fill your heart," he said. "The strength to deal with the negativity. God will give you the light, the hope, and the strength to ensure you can continue your life—with your dad or without him."

He smiled, gripping my hand in both of his. "You are young and smart; you should enjoy the life of a teenager! If your father does not return, you have to be ready to release this negativity from your heart, or it will drag you down and destroy you."

He looked me in the eye. "To combat this, I want you to pray every day, and whenever you feel lost, the church is open to you. I am always here: I am Father Andrea, and I am very happy that you came."

He gestured to the small chapel. "This will be your secret place, very quiet, where you can cry, think, and meditate peacefully without any distractions; no one will see your sadness or know the anguish that you are in. People are too busy with their own lives to focus on your father being missing from yours. They only see what they want to see. But there is one person in your life that cares about you and loves you infinitely. One person who is more special than even your dad, and He will never run away from you. He can be your friend as well, even if others don't care very much about your situation. But God ... He will care about you!"

For the first time, I began to see the light; a hint of happiness was creeping back into my heart. That day was the beginning of my strength. I was the first day I did not feel alone; I was finally calm. The storm was passing, and I could see the flowers around me.

Twice a week, I visited the church, helping the Father Andrea with the cleaning, candles, and mass. He also offered the chance to spread the word of the Bible around our area for about ten euros a day. That positive purpose and influence saved me from depression.

* * *

It was one week until my birthday. I have done my homework. I had some savings from the Bible advertising, and I was now thinking more positively; although the atmosphere was heavy, I tried to stay upbeat.

Mom was ready to talk with me about my birthday. "Honey, you will be thirteen soon! What would you like to do?"

I couldn't help it—I told her the blunt truth. "Mum, you know what I want? I want Dad here with us again. Please ..."

She started to cry. "I want it as well, love," she told me. "I am sorry if I'm not here enough for you as a mother. I am trying, but I am on my own as well!"

I was holding back tears myself, and I didn't want to see my mom cry anymore. Once again, I tried to remain positive. "Mum ... there is one thing that I really want to do for my birthday. I want to go to the car wash and stay inside the car while the car is being washed!

"That's all?" she asked.

"Yes Mum. Please, can we do that for my birthday?"

"Come on Lexi, we don't have to wait for your birthday to do that," she said. "Maybe we could go this coming Friday. Then we will get some take-out and go to the movies!" She beamed at me.

I was very excited by this. "Mum, thank you very much!"

My birthday was on Saturday. I started looking for the movie that I wanted to watch, and my friend Chiara asked me what I wanted as a present.

Suddenly, for the first time in a long time, I was happy, because I knew I was surrounded by people who loved me.

That Friday, I wore my favourite jeans, a hoodie, and trainers. I arrived at the car wash with a glass of Coke in my hand. I was ready to see the show!

To start, the car was lifted up, making it seem like we were flying. Soap started splattering down over the windows, and water sprayed from every direction from the machinery. I took another sip of my Coke. I knew the best part of it was still coming...

The sponges! Yes, time for the sponges!

The brushes cleaned the car up and down; it was like a mix of rain and snow. Five minutes later, the car was lowered to the ground. A maelstrom of air arose, buffeting the car from all sides.

My mom was happy to see me enjoy the simplicity. "Look at you!" she said. "You are so excited!"

She held up her camera and clicked away a couple photos of us. "Happy Birthday my love! I feel grateful to have me here." She looked at me, still drinking my Coke. "So, what movie shall we watch?"

"I don't know," I said. "I'm still deciding between 8 Mile or Titanic. Titanic, I think. Mum, yes, Titanic!"

"Okay then," she said. "Look, I was thinking because you are doing so very well in school, that you can watch Titanic tonight with me and 8 Mile next week. What do you think?"

I almost spilled my Coke. "Yes, Mum! Thanks, I love you!"

Three hours after the movie started, we were still watching it! It was quite sad; I cried openly when Jack died. We finished the movie with a pack of tissues to dry our tears. Then, we went to my favourite Chinese restaurant. We ordered some spring rolls and dumplings. That, chicken fried rice, and some crab and lettuce soup led to a satisfying night. It finished with us walking by the sea and looking up at the stars above our heads.

On Saturday, I received a birthday cake from my school mates, a bag, and a pen with my initials. I also invited my friends to afternoon tea at my house, as I knew a part of my family was going to be there as well. With cakes, candies, good company and pictures, my birthday was perfect.

My mood was high until my phone rang; I had a Nokia at the time. I reached over to grab it from where it was beside me, but I was distracted by my friend playing with the balloons. By the time I got it, the ringing had stopped. One missed call, unknown number; well, it was a bit mysterious, as it was my special day. I kept my phone in my pocket, just in case it rang again…

I was going to the bathroom, and there it went again; I felt the vibration in my jeans' pocket. It was an unknown number again.

I pressed the green button to answer. I listened quietly without saying hello.

"Lexi? Baby? It's Dad!"

My heart stopped. My hands started shaking. "Dad? Where are you? Are you okay? I have been looking for you for two months!"

"Lexi! My love, my darling, I miss you so much," was all he said to that. "Happy birthday!" he added.

I started crying. I couldn't talk anymore; my tears did not allow me to get a word out of my mouth.

"Lexi," he said rapidly, "remember that I love you so much; you do not need to cry. I will come back to you; I will come back soon, because I love you. Be strong, please! I must go now. Be safe Lexi." And he hung up the phone.

After two months of not hearing his voice, all I got was a two-minute phone call. Such a shame! I took the tissues from my bedroom. But I was crying too loudly, and my mom and my grandparents came into the room.

"Alexa? Oh, God! Love, we are here, what happened?"

"Dad called a few minutes ago," was all I could say.

My mom was distressed to see me so upset; as soon as she saw me crying, she started crying as well.

He called me for only two minutes, but with just those hundred and twenty seconds, he destroyed my whole week. Everyone was questioning me about where he was and what number he had called from. He did not mention where he was, just that he was coming soon.

No proof, no evidence, just "happy birthday!"

We telephoned the police and informed them about the phone call. My friends were in the living room. I informed them that the party was over because my dad had just called. Chiara was the only one who persuaded me to continue to enjoy the evening. With a piece of cake in my hands and sad eyes, I thanked everybody and shut the main door, helping my mum with the cleaning. I was still upset. I still could not believe that call.

* * *

Six months later, I received another call, my dad telling me that he was safe and he missed me. He still did not mention when he was coming back and where he was living now. Our calls were full of unanswered questions and awkward small-talk. My father called me only occasionally, maybe six times in a year. Every phone call was about two minutes, with no ID and no locations. Why? Was he a dangerous person? Or was he the one in danger? Had he escaped from someone?

I felt very close to discovering the truth.

2. Sicily and the Mafia

Sicily: a beauty of an island, surrounded by prickly pears (fico d'India) and hugged by the blue of the Mediterranean Sea, with caper-covered caves and naturally-white beaches along its perimeter. The land of love and passion!

Yes, this island is very beautiful. In every moment of my life, I can remember the best of it; every positive moment I spent there was important and full of meaning. You can find a real man there: one who is vital, jealous, authoritarian, passionate about socialising, and just plain awesome.

In Sicily, anything and everything is possible. One day you could choose to be a dentist, or a beautician, a teacher, or maybe open your very own business. As long you know the right people, anything is possible. This is because the art of networking, from a good helping-hand recommendation to bribery and straight corruption is an authentic, "Made in Italy" product! And Sicily is even worse than the rest of Italy.

For most jobs, when you get to an interview, they may claim that you don't have the required skills. But the reality is, the reason you might not be the right candidate for them is not because you are not clever enough, but because you are not the daughter of a particular doctor, or you are not the cousin of the President, or you are not the son of the Minister. If you are not well-connected, they don't want to tell you the real reason, so instead they point to your CV, saying they need someone who speaks German, or they prefer someone who has a pilot's licence. Whatever the reason given, they will always find an excuse for rejecting you—or hiring you!

When I was young, I used to think that maybe the Air Force would be different; that it would be an organization of total integrity: it had the reputation of the government behind it, after all. But even there it was like Sicily, too, and that feeling of perfect morality was only in my dreams.

However, I wouldn't escape Sicily to learn that until much later. And when I did, connections and corruption wouldn't be all I was escaping.

* * *

I was only 13 years old when I first became involved with the Mafia.

I was walking to school: it was springtime. The flowers were in full bloom, and the grass was very new with a fantastic smell of fresh growth. The street was busy with cars backed up by traffic lights. My bag was full of books, and I was totally ready to get an "A" on my essay, because I had been studying very hard all the previous week. I had the feeling that today was going to be a good day.

Suddenly, I noticed that two guys were walking close behind me. They were walking in my shadow, practically close enough to breathe my perfume. I started to walk faster, but they kept pace with me. My legs were shaking, and my heart raced.

Having had enough, I stopped in the silence of the road, turned around, and looked them in the eyes. I was surprised to recognise them; they were the men who had met with my dad before he ran away! Of course I would remember them, because they looked so dodgy.

I did not have time to ask them what they wanted from me before a car stopped next to us and they pushed me inside. Nobody saw what happened to me in those thirty seconds; it's crazy to think that just half a minute changed my whole life.

The road was busy: people were walking to and from the store, the nearby petrol station was full of customers queuing, and the post office was already open. How could nobody see what had happened to me? Did nobody care? Or maybe they knew those guys, and they preferred to pretend not to see and go about their day without calling the police? Or maybe they only saw what they wanted to see. This was my first experience with the Mafia, but I would soon learn. There were three rules with the Mafia: do not talk about it, do not listen to anything about it, and do not share it!

I was on my own, thirteen years old, with nothing but my school bag. My heart jumped into my throat at the terrifying feeling of metal touching my forehead near my right ear. It was a gun! Wait … I knew that gun—that was my father's Beretta .92. How could I be scared of a gun that was so familiar to me? I kept myself calm and relaxed with that thought. Why had they come for me? Was my dad alive, or living elsewhere?

Without saying anything, they drove off with me in their car. I did not cry or act like a baby because I wanted to discover the truth. But make no mistake, this was a proper kidnapping!

In the car, they told me that if I was quiet, it would not been necessary to drug me; therefore I stayed silent and listened to what they were saying.

They took me to the seaside. From the edge of the road, I saw a villa. The wall was white and blue, with a palm tree outside by the car parking. We parked there, and then one of the guys pressed the buzzer. At the gate, a German Shepherd barked viciously as we walked through to the main entrance.

One guy caught my attention: he was smoking a cigarette and held a gun casually in his right hand. He had a rosary around his neck and a scar on his left cheek. Of course I was scared, but I was very curious too. Also, I didn't want to die here with these miserable men. I was confused, and needed answers.

They took me into the main room of the villa, passing by a Jacuzzi and a swimming pool to get there. Luxury was everywhere. The villa was very nice, but I wasn't there to admire the place or the view. They left me to wait in the living room; a lady asked me if I would like something to drink.

"Yes please," I said. "Can I have a Sprite, please?"

"On the way to you," she responded.

It was only half nine in the morning, and the living room was full of glasses and whisky ready to be served … but to be served to who?

Then steps approached the sofa where I sat. A man came over to me … a large man in his forties wearing an expensive suit. Straightening his tie, he came to me and touched my face. "Just like your father," he said. "Beautiful and smart. How old are you now, Alexa?"

"Thirteen, I am thirteen—too young for you," I added.

"I am Giuseppe, but you can call me Toto, or better yet, Padrino Toto."

"Padrino" means "Godfather" in Italian. I was still thinking it over. Who was this guy? What did he want from me? I took a sip of my leftover Sprite.

He asked me, "How is school now? I heard that you are the best in your class!"

When I didn't respond, he added, "Well, I am very confident about you and your strengths: you were always clever, my daughter!"

"My daughter? I am not your daughter," I retorted. "Where is my father? Why have you given him all this stress? What do you want from him? What do you want from me?"

He gave me a placating smile. "Alexa, my darling, your dad is good guy; he just needs a break from his life; sometimes, a man needs time for himself to think. He just needs to take some space, nothing much. Don't you worry about your father: he is proud of you, and I will ensure that you are a respected girl in Sicily. I will make sure that nobody touches you, because they have to go through me first in order to get to you.

He sat on the sofa, one arm over its back. "I don't want to waste your time, as I know you are very busy teenager, but I need a favour—just a favour—from you. You have a scooter, yes? And the police never stop angelic faces like yours."

I look around at this man's grand villa. "What kind of favour?"

"I need you to use your scooter to transport a present for me. After all, I am your father's friend! I would offer you five hundred euros every week if you promise to work for me and do the job properly." He leaned forward, elbows on his knees. "But there is one condition: you cannot get the police involved. No friends either; just you and me."

I paused, watching him for a reaction. "What happens if I refuse?"

"Why would you refuse five hundred euros per week? I think with that money you could support your mother and stay comfortable. You are clever girl, and I need someone like you: someone who could be a team leader, someone who I can trust."

"Yes, Toto," I said, "but I want to think about all you have said. It is tricky work, and I need to be sure before I take it."

He took me to school that day himself. Before I stepped out of the car, he touched my knee and said, "Okay Alexa, don't forget to open your bag after school—there is a present for you!"

I closed the car door and shook hands with him.

I was back in school, but very late. I spoke with the teacher and told her that my lawyer had something important to tell my mother and I, and that's why I couldn't make it to class on time.

"I know, I missed my exam!" I said. "Is there anything that I can do to make it up? Please, I am begging you."

She gave me a stern look and said, "Look Alexa, only for this time! Grab a chair and start your assessment at the end of the tables by the corner."

"Oh, thank you so much," I responded, relieved that I had another chance to get the "A" I needed.

I finished my essay and used the lunch break to go to the gym's changing room. There, I looked inside the bag and found one thousand euros and a card saying:

It was lovely meeting you today, Alexa. I hope we can work together. It is not just for me, do it for your dad as well, as he loves you!

I called my best friend, Chiara, and told her to meet me in the changing room. She came; I showed her the card and the money. I took out a lighter and burned the card, then hid the money in my diary.

That is how my gang life started.

You get a certain kind of respect from people when you walk around like you are important. Unfortunately, this is only what people see from outside, their first impression; but what do they really know of what is behind that image?

I was the first girl my age in high school to drive a scooter. I had a Vespa Piaggio. It was illegal, as it was modified from a 50cc engine to about 125cc. I well remember how I enjoyed the rush of speed and fresh air during the Summer. I also drove it every day to go to school; sometimes I would pick up Chiara, who lived on the other side of the street.

That scooter was everything to me. My family was disappointed in Grandad when he bought it for me; they were worried about the possibility that I could crash and get hurt or killed.

I did not care at all about the risk; the fantastic rush of adrenaline was enough to make me feel alive, and without that, I could fall back into my Black Moon again.

One day, I was driving with Chiara by the seaside. A guy was having a spring bath, totally naked. Chiara and I were admiring his impressive body. I was driving, and didn't notice the broken road in front me because I was distracted. I crashed the scooter and punctured both wheels. We had to walk for about two hours until we reached the first tyre repair shop.

Luckily I was with Chiara that day, and she lent me some money for the repair. Chiara was very close to me; she never let me down. She was a loyal, clever girl, with huge green eyes, black curly hair, and a very calm attitude. She had a strong personality, and she totally disapproved of my involvement in the Mafia. Because she cared about me so much, I shared everything that I was going through with her; she knew all of my weaknesses.

Chiara never judged me: she was there for me, she helped me, and she was very good at keeping a secret.

* * *

It had been a year since my Dad left Sicily—a year of me looking after his deals with Giuseppe. The scooter was a good excuse for me to be independent and reach my friends, do what I needed to do, and get home without arousing attention. But I didn't have a good excuse for the extra money I was earning. Although we had a good lawyer for our case, Dad did not send my mom any money, and I wanted to help. So I decided to work.

My mom did not know about it. She was struggling financially, so she decided to sell her car, a Fiat Panda. I had many memories of that car, including driving home in a storm that damaged the seaside cities of Sicily. That car had given rides to everyone: it was quite small, but very efficient.

Although she sold the car, I did not want to use her money for schoolbooks and my admission fee, so I decided to start working at a bar in the local area. The shop was opposite a church and was managed by a cop, Stefano. He was a sexy cop, very fit: he worked out every day at the gym. Maybe that was the reason I wanted the job so badly. He had brown hair and black eyes, and nice cheeks when he smiled. His arms were massive and dark, and his skin colour was gold: a mix between a good tan and his natural skin tone. He was a regular customer in the tanning shop, since his girlfriend worked there.

When Stefano interviewed me, I told him I was sixteen years old and wanted to work because I loved being independent. He was trained me every day: how to pour a drink, how to make an espresso, how to use the tills; in one week I was ready to go.

He used to pay my wages as 'cash in hand,' as he was aware of my school hours. The job was easy to do, with flexible hours, although the money was not worth the time: I started at 2pm and finished around 8pm. I earned about twenty euros daily, but I could not complain, as I was earning enough for what I had planned.

My daily routine started with me going to School, doing my homework on my lunch break—or any break available, for that matter. I always tried to use the opportunity to review my essays with my brightest schoolmates, those who were more clever than I; sometimes we used their houses or mine to review exams, and in exchange I gave them my scooter for a day during the week, or let them drive it with me.

My mother was working as a Home Help at that time, so she never really knew when I got home. She left for work around 1pm, and that was the time I finished school, ran home to refresh myself, and then off to work. When I got home, I began to get dinner ready for her and help her with the housework. She usually finished around 9pm.

Everything was running as usual until one day my mother started following me. She was looking after me as usual, and our relationship was as normal as any other day. I didn't notice anything unusual.

I was a bit tired that day due to a school project, so I didn't have the time to stop at home as usual. Instead, I decided to take the scooter and drive to work. I started my shift as usual: serving the regulars, those who start to drink whisky at 2pm, and talking about the weather. I already could tell who a new customer was and who was more special. Stefano was at the till, busy with his staff. Everything was as usual, until I saw my mother!

As soon as she walked into the bar, my heart stopped. My cheeks went red and my voice very quiet. I thought to hide myself in the bathroom, but I did not want any trouble with Stefano. I decided to remain calm and see what Mom wanted. She arrived with a friend, but she was not there for a coffee or a drink—she was there for me.

She opened the door and shouted, "I knew it! I knew you were here! Why did you lie to me? What is wrong with you? Are you a homeless person, that you need to work in this dirty bar, surrounded by old men waiting for a chance with you? It is not a proper place for you! Get out now!"

I listened to her concerns, and I tried to tell her that she was wrong: my boss behaved well with me.

As soon as she looked into my eyes, I said, "Mum, please. I must pay the admission fee for school, and I also need new clothes for September. I cannot leave now—I just started my shift!"

She gazed at my boss, then said, "Excuse me sir, do you know my daughter's age?"

Stefano remained polite. "Well, I know she is only sixteen years old, but she is very committed to her role."

"Really?" My mother said. "I am afraid she is only fourteen, and it is illegal to hire a teenager without a contract!"

My boss straightened. "Well, my name is Stefano: I am a police officer. I understand your reaction, but your daughter told me she was sixteen; I am sorry for the mix-up."

She looked him over and took my arm, saying to Stefano, "We are leaving! Goodbye!"

As soon as we were out in the street, she turned her ire on me. "Lexi! Why? This place is not for you! Let's go home."

I tried to protest, but she cut me off. "Let me be a mother to you! I am working really hard to raise you properly, trust me. Since your dad left, everything is on me. But you need to give me an opportunity instead of judging me all the time!"

"Mom, I want to work and be independent, please," I responded.

"Lexi, you are still so young, and this world is too dangerous for you! You are my baby girl, and I cannot put you at risk." She saw my look and softened. "If you really want to work part-time, I know an ice cream place that would be suitable for you; then you will not serve whisky, but ice creams."

That did sound like a better option; Stefano's bar was smelly and dirty, as well as being a bar full of old men. "Yes Mum!" I agreed. "I want to have a chat with the owner of that ice cream place please. I want to have a job! It's been good to have cash in my purse every day."

I did not want to look too suspicious in my mother's eyes—she was not aware of the deal I had made with Giuseppe and my father's friends, and my part-time work was also an excuse for me having money from that. Justifying a lot of cash, especially at my age, was not easy. I needed to work, so at least I could tell her that my boss had decided to give me a pay rise or a bonus or something.

I did have a secure, secret place where I was hiding my cash and the drugs, but she was the kind of mother that could find the impossible.

I wasn't as worried she would find the money as I was that she would find the cocaine. But I had a solution for that as well. Cocaine is easy to confuse with baking powder. So, I emptied some containers of baking powder and replaced it with the White.

For the cash, I could not explain it all with my job; however, I did have a Barbie Doll. Yes, a Barbie: I would cut the silk of her dress with scissors, insert the cash, then fix it by sewing it up again.

My grandmother taught me how to sew. The first time that I tried sewing, she put an orange in my hands and told me to use it as a base, in order to help my finger pass the line with the needle. She also used to put money next to the orange if I would sew with her.

By the end of the year, all of my dolls were transformed. I was very proud, and my family was aware of how protective I was with my newly-decorated toys! They knew that before touching any of them, they had to ask for my permission.

Everything was quite manageable, apart from the guns. It was far more difficult to hide the guns! Particularly because I did not want to separate them from the bullets. In the end, I had to make the difficult decision to involve Chiara. She knew about the guns, and her family had a garage by the seaside that never got used. It was the best place for us.

The first time she showed me the garage, I drove my scooter up to the door. I was carrying a lot of heavy metal; the bullets fell on the garage floor, and when she saw them, she was a bit scared. But we took every possible precaution. It was her idea to install a camera by the main entrance, which I bought.

Sometimes, we would go there and check on the guns. One day, we were drinking a few beers and decided to practice shooting. Chiara had learned to shoot on empty dogfood tins, and with all the practice, we both became pretty good marksmen.

We told ourselves we were quite ready to shoot a person, but we did not want to go to prison; a few of our friends were already there for far too long. We promised each other to always be good girls, find good husbands, and raise a nice family: to be good friends and good mothers.

3. Dealing with Drugs

Cocaine. I lost a lot of friends because they couldn't control this powerful drug. I saw people selling gold, houses, cars, and, in the most uncomfortable situations, even their own bodies. Prostituting yourself for this drug; isn't that cool? No, it is not. Because for the vulnerable, this drug will make them do anything.

The favour Giuseppe asked of me was to use my scooter to become a drug dealer. Which I didn't really want to do for him, but in order to see my Dad again, I decided to collaborate with him. So I started ferrying drugs. I never stored my helmet in the space reserved for it in my little black Scarabeo Piaggio—it was always full of cocaine. I would spend every night of the weekend at the club. Different owners would call me to deliver cocaine to their club to sell.

One day, I was driving from the club to a bar. The road was quiet, and the moon was white and full, like a giant snowball; it reflected beautifully on the sea. I was driving over a bridge, the fresh ocean air pulling at the dress I was wearing, although I had pulled a hoodie over it just to feel comfortable.

I reached the edge of the bridge, where there was a check point on the left side. Police with dogs. A police officer stepped forward, waving a stop sign at me. I decelerated, and it seemed as if my heart stopped along with my scooter. For a moment I felt my teeth chattering, like when you get a high fever. I tried to smile at the officer, who looked very serious and strict.

"Good evening; driving licence and scooter insurance."

"Yes sir, here you are. How are you?"

He didn't answer me. He did, however, notice a pack of Marlboro Lights on my scooter's dash, right behind the windshield. "Your ID says you are only fourteen years old; don't you think fourteen is a little too young to smoke?"

I had to think quickly for a smart answer … I met his eyes with my wide ones. "Sorry sir, I have an exam next week at school, and I am very nervous. The teacher is very strict with the class, you see, and I want to score A+ on it. So sometimes I smoke; I know I am too young. I think I will give up now. You are right, I am too young to smoke."

He gave me a stern nod. "I hope so. Have a good night, and drive safe!"

I turned on the scooter and I drove until I reached the edge of the Piazza. There, I stopped for few minutes, just thinking how lucky I was. My adrenaline raced for few seconds, then I was calm again. I continued my journey, intent on delivering the drugs to the other club.

I waited to get paid the usual envelope of cash, then ducked into the bathroom to check the amount. Two thousand euros and a "thank you" card for being on time. Satisfied, I left the bathroom and walked up to the bar.

There, a young guy started waving at me, calling me by name. He stopped me and kissed my hand. "Hey, you don't go nowhere; you stay here with me, Alexa," he said.

The guy was my neighbour, Patrik: a classy guy who was living the dream, growing up in a rich family; he planned to leave and study in Cambridge when he turned eighteen. Not one for the simple things, he was very Posh and sophisticated all the time.

Patrik insisted on offering me a drink and, of course, I accepted. He was not there by himself: there were a few girls around him, all ready for a line; Patrik always offered cocaine at parties. I didn't care for getting high with it, so instead he offered me a pill he called "MD," also known as ecstasy. I didn't want to take it myself, and his friend was begging me for it, so I decided to get rid of it by handing it to him. Later I saw him dancing in a weird way and shaking his hands, sweating all over and acting like a crazy guy. By the end of the party he was wearing sunglasses in the corner.

The music—techno—was not very good, so while the guys weren't paying attention I walked away. I was still thinking about that guy begging me for some ecstasy, then acting so different from how he usually was. Unbelievable.

Cocaine, it is always there at every party waiting for us, ready to be snorted. If you snort, smoke, or inject cocaine, or you care about someone who does, you more than likely have some unanswered questions about the nature of this powerful drug. Cocaine is an intensely-addictive stimulant that causes dramatic changes in the brain and behaviour. It is common for rich people to use cocaine every day as a recreational drug to get them high.

But what we really know about Cocaine? Crack cocaine is derived from cocaine hydrochloride by taking powdered cocaine and adding ammonia (or baking soda) and heat to remove the hydrochloride and change the pH. This takes it from an acid to its base alkaline form. This process also makes the drug combustible, so it can be easily smoked. The resulting product is then broken into small pieces, or rocks, that can fit into a small pipe, or that can be packed into a cigarette or cigar.

When crack is smoked, it is quickly absorbed into the blood through the lungs. It takes less than five seconds for the entire dose to reach the pleasure centre of the brain. For veteran users, just seeing the crack pipe approaching their lips accelerates this process due to their learned anticipation of the cocaine's effect. Because cocaine reaches the brain so rapidly—before it can even reach the liver—the enzymes designed to protect the body from toxins cannot do so. The resulting "high" is immediate, intense, and very addictive.

When a drug is smoked, the psychoactive effects, potential for addiction, and other harmful consequences are greatly increased. The high from cocaine is determined by the volume of the drug and by the speed at which it arrives at its target in the brain. My friends described a cocaine euphoria that peaks in ten to twenty minutes.

I saw people using cocaine in different ways: chewing, snorting, injecting, and inhaling. Snorting is the most common way to use cocaine. I saw some of my good friends become addicted to it, and they would dissolve the cocaine powder, combine it with heroin, and inject it. I would see them on their journey before, during, and after; it was like they were dreaming, but they were there with me, watching movies or smoking a cigarette. When I looked into their eyes, I understood that this drug can give you the worst sensations.

I will never forget that look; their eyes looked like dead, like when you go to the market to buy fish; in order to buy the freshest one, you have to first check on the fish's eyes. If the eyes are shiny and clear, then it is a good one to get. But if they are dull and dead, you want to avoid them. That was how my friends' eyes looked: dead. Dead like there is no light on, dead like their lives had sunk into a deep depression, dead like they would never smile again. I never tried that drug. I lost so many friends to it, so why would I want to?

So, how did I know if a friend of mine was using cocaine? The first thing I would notice would be a runny nose or frequent sniffles and dilated pupils—so very black that if you were to see a girl with blue eyes doing cocaine, you would be very lucky to see any blue in her eyes at all, as the black pupils would be so dilated that you will not see the colour of her iris.

Another tell-tale indicator was a long period of wakefulness followed by a loss of appetite. Overconfidence was another sign. You can feel so powerful in that hour on cocaine that you could be a CEO for sixty minutes. This drug provides so much stimulation on the day that you use, but the next day, everything changes. Those friends I saw after their high were in a dark tunnel, giving them paranoia, mood swings, irritability, and depression, and often led to them missing or being late to work, financial problems, and even legal issues. The long-term results were never worth the sixty minutes of perceived happiness.

4. Extortion and Escape

The best investors say that any economic crisis will affect a business' investments.

The best extortionists say that the only economic crisis that concerned the business of extortion was the Euro; yes, the change to the Euro in the European Union.

The Lira was the old Italian currency before the Euro was introduced in 2002. Many people in Sicily were struggling due to this change: businesses were failing, and the agricultural industry suffered huge losses. And when Italy flounders, people can survive only if they borrow money from the Mafia; not because they want to ask for money from such horrible people, but because they have no choice: because they have children to feed, but have no job and no money to provide for their family.

So as soon as you are desperate, the Mafia is ready to be your friend, helping at the point when you need them most, then waiting for the opportunity to act like the most vicious of loan sharks. Before you know it, they will give you a deadline: "You have forty-eight hours to find the money—or I will take half of your land! Then your wife, then give your bones to my pit bulls!"

Unfortunately, those words are true. I was there, hearing them alongside a man and his family. And I was the one holding the gun. I had to shoot him; that was my job. It wasn't at all like shooting beer bottles with Chiara.

The bullet shattered his ankle. Blood gushed, and I could see his exposed muscles. I couldn't stand the sight.

Someone told me after, "Alexa, you are too soft; but you will improve, it will just take time. You are smart!"

Since that episode, nightmares have been my closest company while I sleep and nausea frequently wakes me up in the middle of the night.

I was involved, too involved. I could not turn back.

Sometimes, I think if I could only go back in time to that day ... Yes, that day standing in my Father's shop; seeing him talking to those guys. If only I had let my mom know about those dodgy men, and that the gun was missing.

But I kept my mouth shut, just as I did when I was forced to shoot someone who looked like an honest guy: innocent, with a wife and child. I am thankful that in that moment the bullet damaged his leg, instead of his heart. However, the fact remains that they were hurting him so just for a few thousand Euros.

This is the value of a person.

Everyone was already waiting for that man's land. The extortionists were ready to make their profit. Meanwhile, I was by the car, watching his wife and child crying from the window, praying to God for his recovery. Moonlight and cigarette smoke drifted over my skin. The dog barked, and the air was chilling. My reward waited for me there in the car. A reward for keeping quiet, for keeping everything locked deep inside. I was dying to talk about it, but I couldn't talk; they could kill my mom and my grandparents. At the time, I could not think of a good plan; all I knew was I had to finish school first.

The best solution would be to escape, but it wouldn't be as easy as simply leaving; I had to escape in a different way. Maybe I could join the Armed Forces, or the Military Police...

One thousand euros waited for me there; the cost of my silence. As soon as I touched that money, I knew what was meant when they call it "dirty money:" because to earn that quick income, you have to have done something dirty.

Then came the part that chilled me the most; the men I was with started chatting about where they should stop for ice cream and petrol. I was aghast; why were these people talking about ice cream? How could they even think about ice cream after shooting somebody?

That day damaged me; I felt like a part of myself went missing. For those guys, it was like a normal day at work: just nine-to-five, but instead of taking the tube, they take a bike; instead of having pens, they have knives; instead of having laptops, they have firearms.

I experienced another common example of extortion a week later. I was in a massive villa by the sea—a villa so large it would be hard to visit it all in one day. I was in the spa area, where they had a steam room inside the sauna. There, the temperature reached 180 degrees when they closed the entrance. The owner of the villa was inside with his wife.

A few weeks later, that couple was on the Missing Persons list.

In every team, there is always someone new to the group; that person was in charge of cleaning up all the evidence after a crime. They did thorough work; I had my friend's birthday party in that villa a month later, and you never would have guessed that the villa was the last place they had been seen! Six months later, the villa had been sold; the buyer, of course, was Giuseppe.

The Godfather Giuseppe.

I was dying to talk to Chiara about that. But I stopped to think about her health; I didn't want her sleep to turn into nightmares, so I kept it to myself.

I only lie if I need too.

* * *

One day, a seemingly-random guy forced my house door, trying to get into the kitchen. He broke in and took all of my dolls that hid my extra cash in their hand-sewn dresses. The only other thing he stole was the TV, because inside the screen of the TV we kept a camera; a camera that was connected to Giuseppe's TV, so that if I got in trouble he could send somebody to help me.

I saw the thief as he was running away. I was shocked. Who was that guy? How did he know about my secretive dolls? And where the camera was?

Chiara never said a word, but I knew it must have been a friend of hers. I knew her personality and the way she was. I just didn't think she would go this far.

I was wrong. That guy was sent by her, but why?

She wants me to stop with this life.

I was still in shock—how could she do this?—but I knew I could not think about Chiara right then; I had to come up with a plan. Something different than the Mafia's usual response. She was my best friend; I could not hurt my best friend.

Then, I stopped. I saw Giuseppe on his bike, pulling away from my house. I hadn't realized he was in the area—he must have seen the thief running away, too. He told me to jump on the back seat.

"On the back seat ," I asked. "right now?"

"Yes, come on; we have not got much time!" He added.

I did it, of course. Although I saw the direction the guy ran, I didn't want to tell it to Giuseppe; I was sure he would kill him.

It didn't matter, unfortunately. He followed the thief and crushed him with that motorbike. He hit him once, then came back to crush him again and again, running over his bloody skin with his wheels!

"I told you," Giuseppe scolded me, "you need to tell me everything; you cannot hide anything from me. Nobody is going to mess with my daughter! Go home now, try to rest; I know everything with this stupid guy has been traumatic. I am sorry about that, Alexa!"

Sorry? I thought. You got rid of that guy like he was toilet paper, then you say you are sorry... I kept this thought to myself, and walked towards my house like I was told.

Unfortunately for that guy, when he tried to break into my house, Giuseppe was nearby; otherwise, things could have gone differently. Looking back on that day, I mostly just feel guilty.

Giuseppe saw that I was upset with him. He called me; I let my phone ring for a time, then...

"Hello?"

"Alexa," Giuseppe said. "I didn't want that guy around as a witness; please try to understand. Remember this," he added, "it must be done! That guy could not stick around, because he would have put you at risk, Alexa. Information is like a virus, and he will spread it! You would have gone to prison, and then I must visit you there every day. I don't want that for you; you are a good girl, going to school and doing well. Prison is not your future, my love; your Dad would not be happy about it!"

I did not know why he was so protective to me. Personally, I felt a mix of hate and love for him. He made me feel uncomfortable sometimes, but he never touched me in a bad way; he always respected me, and he loved me in a good way.

He met my mother once: he came to see my school assessment. He told my mother that I was very clever, and had done a fantastic presentation. I was quite happy to see him there.

He was always there for me: teaching me how to drive a car, how to shoot, how to eat lobster, how to properly hold the glass while you drink champagne. Teaching me how to check for fake banknotes, how to handcuff a person, and how to play pool.

Many days after school, we would meet, usually just a few minutes for coffee.

Then, when he bought that villa by the sea, he gave me a present. A pool table in his living room. He was teaching me how to play, and gave me the opportunity to enter the Regional Competition; he even came with me to the competition. I know it is not right for me to say it, but for me he was my dad.

I used to have dreams about him; not nightmare, but hot dreams.

He was there for me anytime I wanted.

One Christmastime, he took me to the Cars Expo. Then with his firm voice, he told me, "Choose a car; a beautiful car for a beautiful woman."

The white Fiat 500 caught my eye. A spontaneous smile came to my cheeks.

"Drive it!" he said. "Go for a quick ride! Drive around and see if you enjoy it."

When I returned, he asked, "So, how was it? Do you like the car?"

"Of course," I said.

He spoke with the supervisor for a few minutes, and some money discreetly changed hands. The owner handed me the car keys.

When those keys touched the skin of my palm, I had goose bumps!

I drove around the city in the most popular car; my friends

used to invite me to go to the cinema and go for a walk just because they were in love with my car.

At that time, I realized who my real friend was, who were the fake ones. I saw Chiara a few times at the cinema and at the shop. But our friendship was changing...

I knew Chiara had a plan. So, I decided to use one of those fake friends to check something for me. Since the time that guy broke into my house, I never visited the garage where the guns were hidden. I had a feeling that if Chiara told someone to break into my house, that she would have done something to that garage, too.

The guy I chose to help me was quite fast; he was a marathon runner, and he ran in a lot of competitions around the country. He was quite popular, too. So, I offered to let him drive my car, but only if he could check the inside of the garage for me.

I took him there. It was getting a bit late, right around sunset, but that still gave us enough light to see. I stopped the car. In the silence of the evening, all we could hear was the running noise from the motor.

I looked into his eyes and said, "Are you exited to drive my car? I will take some pictures of you while you are driving."

He gazes at me with a smile. "Alexa, I am glad I have finally met you! You are a very nice girl! Sure, I'll go and do this for you."

He started to walk toward the garage. It took him a couple minutes to reach it. I lost sight of him, but I was sure he was by the door.

He called on my cell phone. "Hello? Alexa, I am here by the door."

"Good!" I said. "Please, open the door."

"I can't," he said. "There seems to be something blocking it from the inside."

"Can you try to push it?" I pressed.

I had given him the key, but he still had to force the door. I heard it open.

"I am in ... what do you need?"

"I just need you to walk around the garage," I said.

As soon as he put his foot on the next piece of the floor, there was an explosion! I heard it clearly from the car.

I called Giuseppe and informed him about the accident. He sent two big men to clean up the evidence, then sent that guy I had asked to enter the garage to the hospital. He was paid to stay quiet.

In the morning, I drove to Chiara's house before school. I stopped my scooter in front of her house, and waited there for her to come out. I saw her parents leave the house, walking towards their car. They left, and a few minutes after I saw her.

I took my helmet and held it against Chiara's head. "How could you do that to me?"

I started crying. She was the only one who could really hurt me; she held a part of my heart.

For a moment, I thought about our fifteen years together, all those beautiful memories, then of that explosion in the garage. "I could be dead! What is wrong with you?" My voice was raised, but I didn't care. "I am your sister; I know I involved you in this, and I am so sorry, but I cannot stay a minute without you, Chiara. I am lost without you..."

We were best friends; she was like a sister to me. People often thought we were in a relationship, because our fighting was like that of a couple when they argue about stupid things.

With tears on my eyes, I continued to tell her, "I did not walk into that garage; it wasn't me. Would you really want to see my blood on the floor? If I'm to die, I'd prefer you do it, not someone or something else. You have the balls, Chiara!" I gave her my Beretta .92 and told her to kill me: to look into my eyes until I was dead.

She could not hold that gun for even one moment!

Then she said, "Do you understand that you will go to prison? Do you really want this for your life? To die behind the bars—is that what you really want? What about our friendship?" There were tears in her eyes now too. "I want you at my eighteenth birthday party; I want you there when I buy a car, or when I become a mother; I want my friend back. I don't know you anymore, Alexa! Who are you? My friend, or a criminal? You've gotten yourself brainwashed by those gangsters."

She crossed her arms. "You have to choose. Me, or them?"

"Chiara, listen: please don't ask me to do something I cannot do. I am so involved now. But I have a plan."

"Really?" She starts shaking, she is so angry. "You told me that already! No more excuses, Alexa. Please go—get out of my sight!"

I was heartbroken. Chiara … she was the only happy thing in my life. I did want to stay with her, not with them. However, I had obligations with those criminals.

I decided to talk with Giuseppe about how I was feeling. Late one evening, I drove to his house. I saw the sofa again, the sofa where I had that first Sprite a long time ago. And there I was: sitting on that sofa again.

Giuseppe came to join me, and I was ready to talk.

"Alexa, my love, how was school?"

"Toto, listen…" My legs were shaking, I was so nervous. But I cannot hold it in anymore. "I am not here to talk about school; I am here because I don't feel comfortable with you and your team anymore. I am young, I want a better life; I am sorry, but I want to get out of this. Kill me, if is that what you want—"

"Alexa, darling," he interrupted, putting his right hand on my shoulder. "I don't want to hurt you or kill you; why are you saying that?"

"Well, you already did!" I exploded, my fists clenched. "My mental health has been murdered since I started working for you."

"If you don't want this life anymore, it is okay," he said. "Don't worry, I am not upset. I understand. I will, however, talk to your dad about his naughty daughter!"

"Whatever!" I said. "I do not care anymore; please, you can even take back the car if you want!"

As soon as I stepped out the door, I called Chiara.

"Hello?" she answers.

"Hi, it's me. Are you okay? Where are you? I need to see you, and give you some good news."

I walked to her house, which was about forty-five minutes away. I went through a few cigarettes during the walk. Chiara was there, like the groom waiting for his bride at the altar.

I smiled, then ran towards her. "I have done it! It's what you wanted, right? I am out of this; I want to stay with you, Chiara. I choose you! Are we still friends?"

She started crying.

"Come on, don't cry; you should be happy about it!"

She could not seem to talk, and I started to get worried. "Chiara? Chiara!"

Then she found her voice. "Alexa, my father's shop, his shop ... is..."

"Chiara, please tell me, what happened?"

"His shop is gone!"

"What do you mean, 'gone'?"

"Someone put a bomb in his shop; he is at the police station now."

I didn't say a word; I just took my scooter and drove to his shop. I got in, although the firemen told me to keep out. Everything was burning, and the flames were still too high to look for evidence. However, walking behind the shop, I noticed a motorbike driving away from the store.

That motorbike was Giuseppe's bike.

Chiara was devastated, and didn't come to school for about a week; she also didn't want to talk to me at all anymore.

I went to Giuseppe's house. I didn't know who I was anymore, or what I wanted; I was just walking down the middle of the street. I had lost my focus.

Who am I? I kept asking myself.

I opened the front door of Giuseppe's house. He walked to the door to see who had arrived.

"I am here!" I announced.

"Oh, what a surprise?" He let the statement hang, a smug smile on his face.

"Why did you set fire to Chiara's dad's store?" I demanded. "She is my best friend; you knew that."

"Alexa, remember, she was the one who put a bomb in that garage. That is not the act of a friend; she must pay for it!"

I threw my hands in the air. "Toto, can you please stop being a judge? Why do you decide who must pay or not? Now she does not talk to my anymore! Are you happy now? Do you think I will change my mind because I am on my own? I am not scared of being lonely."

Once again he played the role of diabolic manipulator. He opened a bottle of champagne and poured us a couple drinks. It was something he did when talking business.

"Alexa, I see you care about Chiara. I have a plan to help, as we are friends as well. We are friends, aren't we? I will give your friend some money for the shop, enough money to make sure her dad can re-open the business."

"Sure, but what does that mean you want from me now? I know you; I know you will not do something for nothing."

Giuseppe took a sip of his champagne. "Well, there is something that I need. One last job, a last favour. I need you to drive from one city to another and transport some people with you."

"Is it going to be the absolute last job?"

"Of course! Consider it a favour for your friend Chiara. Are you going to go dry her tears now?" He smiled mockingly.

"Have a good night!" I responded. Then I walked away.

The road was quiet. I stopped at a gas station and put some petrol in my scooter, thinking about what my new life could be, and how to look for a way to leave my current dangerous one.

I only had six more months of school, then I was free to plan my escape. So, I kept my mind set and calm, and I agreed to do one last job for Giuseppe.

I had enough money to buy a house, or to go abroad—maybe study in New York. A lot of dreams came into my mind, and a positive feeling that I could actually escape Sicily.

Chiara's text shattered my mood:

Alexa, I have received some money from Giuseppe. What does he want from you? What has he asked you this time? I don't think I can accept this money.

I responded to her:

Please keep the money. I will do anything for you; I will die for you! Don't worry, you can leave it to me: I am on it! Goodnight.

She texted back:

Alexa, while my dad was at the police station to report the fire, the officer told him that there is an online application to join the police! I think it could save your ass from everything!

What? Me in the police? Are you crazy? Go to sleep. Talk tomorrow.

Listen to me, I will help you apply. They will send you far away from Sicily—it will be good for you! It is also a good salary... You already know how to use a gun, don't you? Come on, you said you will do anything for me!

It's late! Let's go to sleep. Night.

* * *

In March of 2008, I was driving a van from Tirana to Italy on a Saturday night. Inside the van were two guys from Albania; it was my job to take them from the border to Sicily. Each of them were paying about ten thousand euros to get into Italy. A guard at the border check point already had an agreement with Giuseppe.

But that guard was not there that night.

I have five kilos of cocaine in the trunk, hidden inside the spare tyre, fifty thousand euros in cash, and three guns.

The guard told me to stop. I smiled, trying to act normal; I did not want to look suspicious.

However, I was already thinking about my life behind bars for the next twenty years. I thought about how I would need a good lawyer, how this would affect my mom, my grandparents, and all the other people who loved me: who turned my negative days into positive ones.

Stupid! I was a loser, exchanging my life for money. I felt so stupid! I think, That's it! This is what I deserve! This is how my life will end.

I stopped the van and gave my ID to the guard. The guard called over a dog for an inspection. My heart stuttered, then stopped.

I will never forget that day. That day, I was the luckiest person in the world!

Behind my van, there is a truck with a family. Suddenly, the guard noticed some people hidden away behind the truck. They made a run for it!

The guard quickly handed me back my passport, telling me to turn the van back on and go. He even apologized to me.

I smiled and said, "That is okay. Have a nice day!"

I lit up a cigarette and looked back on the road from the rear view mirror. I was lucky, God was with me, and Chiara as well, I guess.

I took the Albanians to Giuseppe's house to receive the usual envelope. He was surprised to see me.

I walked to his door and stopped by the mat, as we agreed the job was done. I didn't mention about the guard not being there. I knew that had been his plan! He had tried to make me vanish with that favour. I took the envelope. Five thousand euros inside, not a penny more. Of course, he hadn't even thought I was coming back to Sicily.

I have one month left before I graduated, and I was focusing on studying.

Chiara was acting differently with me. Every day, she pushed me to join the Police. She would stop me in the middle of school, in the bathroom, in the store, saying, "Alexa, I don't see your name in the list? Did you apply for it, or not yet?" Her pressure was as insistent as my mother's pressure for me to earn my GED.

I stopped one afternoon at her house with my passport and my personal details. I rang her doorbell. "I am ready!" I said.

She opened the door and helped me complete the application; not just because she wanted to help me, but also because she wanted proof. Yes, she had to be sure her friend Alexa had finished the application and that it would be submitted.

Soon we received the confirmation email. My application had been submitted.

She hugged me, saying, "I will pray for you; I know they will accept you, I am confident!"

Six months later, I had passed the GED and graduated.

I also got an email saying that my application was successful!

I went to Rome for my interview. I passed the exams and the different tests. Then they checked my height, my mental health, and a general physical exam. They asked if I smoke, drink, or use drugs.

My tests were all fine!

Two weeks later, an envelope arrived.

Ms. Ferilli Alexa, we would like to inform you that your application has been successful. Therefore, we would like to invite you to pack your luggage and attend your first day in the Military Police Training based in Rome.

We look forward to welcoming you on board.

Kind regards,

The Military Police Team

After receiving that letter, my whole family was very proud of me! My mom organized a party, and Chiara and I drank so much that I fell into the swimming pool. And although she wasn't as drunk as I was, she joined me! Her message was clear: If you jump, I will jump with you, because you are my friend.

One week later, I bought a one-way bus ticket to Rome.

Two weeks later, I was wearing a uniform and had a gun.

5. Military Life

I was standing outside my dorm late one night at the Aviano Air Base where I was stationed. I felt the wind tug at my hair. I decided to light up a cigarette; the strong smell reached the window of my co-worker, who he joined me straight away.

"Are you Alexa?" he asked, "from Sicily?

I gaze at him. "Yes, I am; why?"

"Nice to meet you; I am Federico," he said. "People have been talking about you: I heard you were the best female pool player in Sicily."

I shrugged. "Well, I am not as good as I once was, but I can still play."

"There is a pool table over the American side; shall we go there?" he suggested. "It is only a ten-minute walk."

I paused; my eyes were looking at his lips and he looked back at mine. I had only seen him twice before in the canteen. But he was a very handsome guy, this Federico: he was in his late twenties, from Naples; a common Italian fashion guy. His cheeks were chiselled, like a finely-carved Michelangelo statue. His nose was perfectly symmetrical. His lips were slightly full: the kind that end in a cute little smirk at the corners.

"Okay, sure," I said. "Let's go!"

Walking together for those ten minutes was a nice experience for a female Airman. It was still my first week in Aviano after my military training, where I was surrounded by only women over a period of eight weeks.

Aviano Airbase was in Pordenone, in northern Italy. It was divided into two sides: an Italian side, controlled by the Italian Air Force, and an American side, which hosted the United States Air Force.

Aviano was right at the foot of the Dolomite Mountains, and every soldier who was assigned to Aviano Air Base, Italian or American, visited the Piancavallo ski resort there. Sunsets in Aviano were like postcards that you buy from the store, and every moment you missed your family or were feeling a bit down, all you had to do was look up. Every move you made, the landscape was there, like it was talking to you: a huge mountain surrounded by sunlight, blue sky, and white snow, creating vibrations of emotion in your heart, making you feel blessed that you were there.

That was the only thing I really enjoyed about.

Aviano had not been part of my plan; my commanding officer determined my destination during my training, and I really could not change his mind. He thought that experiencing the countryside, far away from my family, would be a good experience for me and encourage me to grow. I was not happy when I first arrived: I had to carry three pieces of luggage to the second floor by myself, and the boys just looked on, following after me; the only person who asked me if I need help was Federico.

I was the second Female Airman in all the Italian Air Base, and all the soldiers tried to flirt with me: during the performance of the National Anthems, during lunchtime, or during the running competitions. Although they were good-looking boys, once you fell into one soldier, you became popular: not because you had won a medal but because you were too easy to get.

I was there only to achieve my goals: to have an extra point for my CV, so I would be able to join the State Police later. I was not interested in flirting, as I had already a plan in mind: if I were going to flirt, I would only be interested in doing so as part of a new experience, such as going to the American side of the base and find a guy for me there!

From the edge of the road, I saw the bar. American flags were everywhere, and parked outside was a Harley-Davidson surrounded by Ford Mustangs. There was a distinct smell of American perfume around the place: a mix of Victoria's Secret body spray and Busch beer. There were a bunch of American girls in short skirts talking about daily bullshit, walking about like they didn't care.

We entered the bar, and I headed straight for the pool table.

There, I was distracted by another good-looking guy. He was playing pool with a couple of friends. He looked Indian, with tattoos over his arms, a rosary necklace, and a NY hat. He was in a bull tank and Nike shoes.

How was it possible for an Indian guy to look so American?

His eyes were beautiful: a very deep brown, with lashes so long and thick it looked like he had mascara on. I was already more than interested.

I started and quickly looked away. Oh my God, I thought. Was he watching me at my table?

Federico was watching me, and caught the coy smile that crossed my lips. "Alexa?" He paused. "That guy keeps looking at you: do you like him?"

"Who?"

"Come on Alexa," he chided me. "Don't freeze me out."

"Not really my cup of tea," I tell him. I lied, of course; I wanted to maintain a level of professionalism at the Airbase.

But it was evident. So Federico gave me a grin and wandered over to talk to him. The music was loud, and there were a lot of people talking, so it was too noisy for me to understand what they were saying. But I understood the body language.

The Indian guy left the pool table. Was he coming toward me? I thought to myself, *Okay Alexa, relax. You can talk in English, can't you?*

Well, I only studied it in high school, and even then the teacher was only interested in Harrods Department Store and Britain's red double-decker busses. So why did I learn it? Because I like Harrods or the red busses?

No. I mean, the previous teacher was cool. She could engage the class, and had the power to immerse us in adventurous stories of the Loch Ness Monster. I always felt like there really was a monster living there, maybe because the lake was dark, like getting lost in a deep, dark sky at 3am.

But even before that, I was always interested in learning English. Eminem was my favourite rapper, and an English point of reference for me, especially when the movie 8 Mile came out. I remember when my mom took me to the cinema for my birthday. She waited outside for me, and as soon as I came out, asked, "Lexi, how was the movie?"

At the time, I found I could not properly express my enthusiasm for what I had just watched. So all I ended up saying was, "Yes, Mum, it was good. Thanks!"

I was always attracted to the street life of the American gangster, especially Eminem, a white rapper.

I took a deep breath. I felt ready to talk. *Okay, calm down, I think to myself. I know I can do it! Just stop talking to myself and try.*

He stands in front of me. "Hi, I am Jason," he says. "Nice to meet you! What is your name?"

I gaze at him. *Oh my God!* Was it a miracle? It was just like a dream come true! I could smell Johnson's baby cream for a second, coming from his skin, but no ... that wasn't the smell. What was it? Palmers cocoa butter lotion—that smell was cocoa butter!

I gave him a hesitant smile. "Jason?"

"Yes! I would love to play a round with you." He takes my hand. "Come with me, let's get a drink first."

Still holding my hand, he took me up to the bar; I was thinking of ordering a Jack and Coke.

There was a relaxed, cool atmosphere at the bar. People were dancing and laughing along with the lyrics: *Down down, do your dance, do your dance...*

When the song started, Jason invited me to dance before getting our drinks.

At first I wasn't going to: I didn't know the song, and I wasn't drunk enough to start dancing in the middle of a crowd. But Jason encouraged me. "Just go to the left when they say 'left,' and to the right when they say 'right'!"

And just like that, I was in the middle of the bar, surrounded by so many different people. I just tried to copy them—this was my first time dancing to this song!

Apparently, it was a very popular American song. "It's the Cupid Shuffle," Jason shouted over the music, *down down, do your dance...* "No worries; you will be ready for it next time when you come back! The DJ plays it every Friday night."

After the song was over, we walked up to the bar counter once again. I'll never forget what that bartender looked like: he was a very big guy, with dark eyes and a long scar on his bald head; when I saw him, I couldn't stop thinking about Uncle Fester from the Addams Family.

"Excuse me sir!" Jason said. "Could you give us two Jägerbombs?"

"Sure!" the bartender answers.

I stop. What was inside this cocktail; was it even a cocktail? With Red Bull?

While I sat there confused, Jason paid the bill of thirteen dollars. "Are you teasing me?" he said. "Come on, don't you know what Jägerbombs are?"

I paused. "Of course," I said. "It's Jägermeister and Red Bull." But I could only say that because I had just seen the bartender pour them.

He smiled and changed the subject. "So, I heard you are a good pool player. Do you know how to play bank?"

This time my smile was confident. "Yes, I play bank as well."

We started off playing handball a few times before the game. Handball is open table, where you can play the white ball wherever you want. Five of the striped balls are played on the table. I got all of them in the hole straight away.

Jason was shocked! The surprise on his face made his eyes even more beautiful than before. I could not stop looking at him and imagining how it would feel to have sex with him on the pool table. I get a bit of a dirty mind while I play.

I won the first game, and Jason' friends teased him relentlessly for it.

We were still drinking. I saw Federico flirting with two Americans. However, it was getting late. I called out to him, "Federico! Federico, I'm leaving."

Federico came over to me right away. "Okay, I am coming with you, let's go!" Once we were walking outside in the dark, quiet night back to our half of the base, he asked, "Alexa? So, how was the game with Jason?"

"It was good, thanks; but why did you talk to him about me without checking with me first?" I was too happy with how the night had gone to be anything more than mockingly angry at him.

He paused at that, then said sheepishly, "Alexa, I gave him your number ... sorry, I hope you don't mind."

"What?" I panicked. "How could you? At least double-check with me?" I was not upset because he had given Jason my number; I was just worried about how I would communicate with him while writing in English... "Okay, it's – it's fine. But next time, please ask me!"

We reached the steps of the dorm. I was on a second floor; Federico stopped on the first. "You are a good pool player," he said. "and hot!"

I bite my lip and gave him a spontaneous kiss on the cheek. "Goodnight Federico! See you tomorrow."

"Goodnight Alexa!"

In my dorm, on my bed, I was still thinking about Jason. How it would feel to kiss his rosary necklace over his skin ... of his body over my body! A mysterious world full of passion, different cultures, and different lifestyles.

I checked my phone.

1 New Message. New number starting with ...

I was feeling sleepy and skipped right to the message:

Hi Alexa! This is Jason! I really enjoyed playing pool with you. Maybe we can play again next Friday? Have a good night!

I replied:

Hi Jason, I am happy that you had a good time. Sure, text me when you are going, and I will try my best to be there! Goodnight!

I was thankful to Federico; this wouldn't have happened if he hadn't given Jason my phone number.

Early the next morning, I was late for the Anthem. Yes, it was Saturday, and it was 8am—actually 08:01am.

I was one minute late, but everyone glared at me as if I were ten minutes late!

It was something that I hated about the military: in the first year, you are committed to singing the National Anthem as the flag is raised over the edge of the building. Every morning, for three hundred and sixty-five days, you have to wake up and walk five minutes to reach the square, where you will admire the flag and sing in a strong, clear voice. If you missed it, you then had to clean the toilets or serve as the gopher for a higher-ranking soldier for the day!

I was tired—I only slept for about 2 hours, and my eyes were heavy. The commanding officer came up to me. He was in his early thirties, with blond hair, sunglasses, and an expression that said you dare not look into his eyes. "Ferilli!"

"Yes sir!" I said.

"Twenty-five push-ups. You were late!"

I nodded my head and dropped to the floor. It was already a hot day, and the asphalt was burning hot. I spat into the palms of my hands. I thought of a torture for the officer, but that would not help me with the push-ups.

I started, but by my first fifteen, my arms were shaking; I could feel the vibration of them against the warm ground.

The officer saw that I was struggling to continue. He put his left boot on my neck, pushing downwards toward the ground. He snapped at me, "You are not a female, you are a soldier! Go away! Now!"

In that moment I felt raped without ever being touched!

I went upstairs to my room again, thinking how it would be in the other side of the Airbase.

The Italian dorms were very old: dark green walls, neglected lawns, bare rooms with only metal wardrobes, spiders on the floor, mosquitoes around your room, and the toilets ... well, the toilets were okay: three showers and three sinks.

I had a rota with the only other woman on base, Maria: we shared the bathroom and the corridor cleaning as well. She was married, and very focussed on her career. She was a very meticulous person; in her spare time, she was only interested in exercising and studying.

One time, I decided to invite her to come to a party. I introduced my friend Federico to her. After a couple of drinks, she was kissing Federico and letting him touch her big breasts. At first I felt a little guilty, because I was aware of her marriage, but she was happy and having fun for the first time; she was really enjoying the night. I was quite happy for her, as she was a classic housewife that looked after her husband, prepared the dinner, and got ready to listen to his parents' problems. I never saw her smiling and laughing like that; so, why should I feel guilty? In the end it was her life, and she was mature enough to understand her limits.

Maria was 5' 6," with curly hair and a shapely body. She wore blue jeans that night and a white top. By the time we returned to the dorms again, the moon was huge and there were stars everywhere. Maria took hold of my hand and looked me into my drunken eyes, telling me, "Alexa, I am so lucky to have you here in my life; since I met you, my life in Aviano has been changed!"

"Well, Maria," I say, "I think you deserve to be happy!"

Being a soldier is a mix of feelings: one day you miss home, and the other you feel at home!

I hug her and wait at my door to make sure she reaches hers.

Lie down on my bed with some hot camomile tea, thinking about the night. My eyes shut almost immediately.

* * *

By Friday morning after my pool date with Jason, I had been checking my phone steadily for three days; no text message from Jason. I hated that feeling when I was checking my phone every five minutes, looking to see if he had texted me; wishing to hear that small tone and see the number that I wanted so badly to see.

I even went to check to be sure that the Wi-Fi was working. The network was fine, the connection was fine! I had been hoping for a text from Jason all day, but I received nothing. I was a bit upset, so I texted Federico to see what he was doing. I wanted to go out, to forget about the disappointment of not receiving a message.

Federico was in his room. He invited me to a party—an American party! I hoped I would see Jason at it, so I decided to wear a yellow dress with silver heels and a silver clutch. Federico had a Mercedes, so I wasn't too worried about having to walk or not drinking, as he was driving.

We reached the club. The music was loud; security at the gate said it was hip-hop and reggae that night. I looked Federico in the eyes and nodded at him, as I wanted to check out the club. We got in and reached the bar. There was no sign of Jason. I was happy to have something familiar, so we each had a couple of shots of Jack Daniels.

I was feeling a little drunk and started dancing close to Federico; his hands followed my movements, and we were laughing and enjoying the music, keeping a few shots on the side for later. The atmosphere was perfect, and we both looked stunning. This earned us the attention of the Americans: they looked at us like we were different. It is a funny thing that I like about Americans: they don't care about fashion or matching one's top with their shoes or their purse with their jeans; they are just comfortable. I would say too comfy for my style. I am not a fan of big brands like Gucci, Chanel, or D&G, but I love to spend time on matching the colours and styles of my clothes.

By then we were in the middle of the disco club, and I was enjoying my dance. A guy came up to me and asked if Federico was my boyfriend. I said, "Yes, he is my boyfriend," and gave Federico a cheeky kiss on the lips. Now uninterested in me, the guy walked away.

"Alexa?" Federico said. "What a lovely surprise from you! How beautiful it is! Can I have another?"

"Federico please," I said, "it was just to make that guy walk away!"

But he was not satisfied with my answer, and suddenly he kissed me, again and again. We were like magnets the whole rest of the night; we couldn't stop touching each other.

We left the club and reached the car in the parking lot. It started raining, but I didn't care, because Federico was there holding my hand, kissing me passionately under the open sky. We were lost in a bubble of time and space, not even noticing the heavy rainfall pouring down over our bodies, soaking us through.

We decided to continue the night together in his room. He took off his T-shirt. His body was perfect: all the right muscles at the right points. He offered me a foot massage. I was super-tired, and fell asleep on his chest. I felt safe and supported with him.

We slept together all night without even thinking about having sex. We took off our clothes and were naked under the blankets, holding each other tight, like two bodies turning into one, and that's how we fell asleep.

Federico was always a part of my life throughout my military career: we had missions together, we had been in different places together, and although we had always been attracted to each other, we never felt it was the right time, or had the effort to dedicate more of that feeling on just us. We were ready to protect the world together, and we were often the leaders on a team, pushing each other to achieve goals, ambitions, and dreams. He even saved my life once in firearms training!

He left me with a lot of good memories, ones that are infinitely better than photographs, as they are safe in my mind; I can see and feel them whenever I want. Those moments are all very emotional for me.

When I finished my training, I was ready to settle down with Federico. Unfortunately, my plans were changed again; another call, this time from NATO, asking me to be posted for six months in Afghanistan.

I kept Federico's picture in my wallet for the entire six months.

But up of my return, I found that with the passage of time, lives change, people change, and plans change as well. As soon as I left my final mission, I tried to call him. But he wasn't in the military any longer; it was his dream came true, he had made it! He was finally in the Polizia di Stato, the Italian State Police, which had always been Federico's goal.

Of course, I was happy for him, but at the same time I was sad, because I knew I had lost him. I had lost an opportunity, like missing that special train that only passes once in your life! I lost that opportunity to tell him about my feelings simply because I was scared or embarrassed. I had not been ready before, but by the time I was, he was no longer there for me.

Federico will be always in my heart. And that picture is still in my wallet!

6. Jason

I will never forget those nights when I used to work at Gate 9. Gate 9 was the worse shift ever in the Air Force—we had to work for twenty-four hours in one shift. Yes, that's right: twenty-four hours on, then twenty-four hours off! Many times, I thought torture must surely be better than Gate 9.

The shift started at 9am in the morning. I would check ID for three hours and inspect every vehicle going in or out. I would have to check that their documents were registered in the airbase and ensure the health and safety of the space.

At noon, someone would pick me up and take me to the canteen for lunch. Then there was training for an hour in the training room; there would often be a briefing with the team, then I would go back again at 3pm to finish at 6pm. I was allowed to stop and have some dinner, and go back at 9pm until midnight.

At midnight I could rest for a few hours, but only on one condition: I could not remove my boots, and the bullets must always remain on my belt with my firearm. Finally, there were the last three hours, from 3am to 6am. In that time, I felt tired, nervous, and hungry, but we were still expected to be vigilant and protect the entrance to the base. So, I would take coffee with me, and few cigarettes that I could sneakily light up once everything was really quiet.

The shift was very organized: one Italian, two Americans. The Americans were always nice to me, and they treated me with respect every time we shared a shift together. The funniest thing about working with them was having some fried egg and peanut butter leftover around 4am. After a long shift, I could not wait until that time, because I was too tired to think and it was cold outside, especially in winter.

One Friday, at 3 am in the morning, the temperature was minus 15, and I had to stay outside by the gate, far away from the heater. I couldn't feel my feet anymore, couldn't talk properly; I could only look at the soldiers coming through the gate and check their ID with my gloves on and with my scarf over my neck.

I saw a BMW coming through to me, and I was ready at the check point. Check point procedures were quite strict—I even needed to check the alcohol level of the driver. If the result was positive, I would have to handcuff him and wait until the police arrived to make an arrest and fill out the other paperwork.

Can you imagine arresting someone at 4am in the morning, and then talking to them and the police after you have stood around for about twenty-two hours? It is not easy, since you reach a point of tiredness that you lose concentration and have trouble with keeping a true perception of reality; the only thing you can think of is your bedroom and a hot drink.

However, that night was different. As soon I pulled over the BMW at the check point, I could see that the guy was familiar to me. He was looking tired too, and I blearily asked him for his ID. I checked his ID and the picture, and of course I knew him—it was Jason!

He was looking cool and immaculate in his uniform. Immediately, I forgot about my previous eighteen hours of shift; the only thing that consumed me was an adrenaline rush of excitement.

It was all coming back to me; yes, my blood was circulating properly again, I was feeling normal and fresh once more, as if there were sunlight heating the surface of my skin.

"Alexa! The pool player!" Jason said in surprise.

"Hi Jason! How are you? It has been a long time since I did not hear from you … I thought you were going to confirm the time for our next game!"

"I am so sorry," he said, lowering his gaze. "I flew to Spain for a two-week mission; I came back yesterday. I was very busy with the training, please forgive me. You don't deserve my silence!"

Distance doesn't separate people, silence does, and I was glad to receive his apology for it.

"What about if we go for a drink tomorrow?"

"Tomorrow?" I hesitated. In my mind I thought that Sunday would be more suitable, but I was so into him that I simply say, "Yes!

That's fine! What time?" I added

"How about 4pm."

"Well, I might still be in bed for 4pm but yes, why not?" I returned his ID, touching his hands with my gloves.

He moved the car and drove through the gate, waving from his window.

My colleague, the American, noticed my suddenly happy face; he saw me standing on my own, smiling, and asked me if I was okay.

"Oh yes!" I said. I was feeling excited about that shift! Gate 9, which I used to hate so much, had now given me the opportunity to start dating the guy that I was into. I could not believe that in about ten hours I would be with my Jason once again!

I was thinking about my nails and my hair; so, I booked a manicure and pedicure straight away! I didn't think about resting, as I had too much adrenaline energising me during the day; so instead I dedicated my time in choosing what dress to wear, what shoes to match with which bag ... the morning ended up quite busy, getting everything perfect and ready for our first official date.

At 3:45pm I was ready; I had done my hair and put on all my makeup. Then I received a text.

Hi Alexa, I am on my way. I will be by your dorm at 4pm.

I got a big smile when I saw that text. I finished putting on my perfume.

While I was drinking a coffee, he called to tell me that he was downstairs waiting for me. He was wearing a black t-shirt, jeans, and Nike shoes, with that same rosary over his neck and tattoos crossing his arms. He hugged me; not those long hugs that you wish to enjoy, but one of those quick hugs that last just for few seconds.

"Hey, how are you doing? You look amazing!" he added.

Well, I had better—it took me about three hours to choose the right outfit for that special occasion.

He turned on the car, constantly looking at me out of the corner of his eyes.

I was feeling good there with him: the music was perfect, the atmosphere warm, and his car was quite comfortable. He put on the seat warmer for my seat, asking me if I felt cold; he was very protective of me that day.

When we reached the restaurant, he pulled into the parking lot and said proudly, "Here we are!" He opened my door, holding my hand.

"Oh, thank you," I responded.

The restaurant was by the mountain; he had booked a place on the terrace where we could see the sunset from the windows.

Jason removed my coat and took with his to leave with the host. Then he ordered a bottle of wine and some olives with some chicken wings.

We began drinking and getting to know each other. He told me that he was originally from Pakistan, and that he grew up in New York City. He left home when he was eighteen years old, and he had been in the Air Force for about four years. He was very happy to stay in Europe, because his plan was to visit Italy, France, Germany, and Malta. He added that his contract would be another two years longer, then he would have to return to the States.

I told him about myself, my ambitions, and my goals. However, my English was not very fluent. Jason tried to help me when he saw I that I was struggling with some words. It took me about twenty minutes just to say where I was from and what drink I usually like!

Yes, this is how everything starts.

He was curious about my lifestyle; I wished I could talk more, but talk I cannot. Yes, I was struggling and was embarrassed.

Smoking a cigarette outside, he asked me if I liked the sunset.

"Yes," I said, "I love the sunset when you can admire the landscape of Piancavallo."

He mentioned that he got stunning mountain views at home from his balcony. So with a cheeky smile I said, "It would be lovely to see it right now..."

Of course, a few glasses of wine in, I was feeling not as shy as I usually was.

Jason got his car from the parking lot, paid the bill, and we drove towards his house. He was still looking at me, and I wanted to kiss him so badly. His lips looked soft and perfect, especially whenever his cute smile crossed his cheeks. He was also about six feet, so it felt good to be walking next to him into the main entrance of his house.

His house was massive: the Aviano Air Base gave about one thousand dollars towards rent to all the American contractors, and he was one of them. There was a swimming pool in the garden, a pond with red fish, a space dedicated to a relaxation with a private bar, two showers by the pool, and a tennis table by the parking.

He walked me in and gave me the grand tour of his home. The living room was spacious enough for about six people. The dining room was by the kitchen in an open space between it and the living room. With two bathrooms, you might expect that one of them would just be a very small one. Not at all; they were both were super huge. The only difference was that one had a Jacuzzi inside, and the other a shower with waterproof radio and speaker. He showed me the bedroom, too. The bed was so high that you could injure yourself if you fell off. The house was super clean.

Jason took me onto the balcony. He set out two chairs for us, and started telling me about the neighbourhood and the shops in the local area.

He handed me a glass of Jack Daniels and I added some Coke to it; we were still chatting, but we moved inside.

It was about 9pm at night, and I was starting to feel tired. I knew that I was off the next day, but I could not keep my eyes open.

He saw me chilling in his living room and offered to let me stay over. But as a first date, I felt I should not even be in his house. It was bad enough I had teased him by asking to see the sunset from his balcony.

So Jason dropped me off at the base again. Holding my hand, he asked me for another date on Tuesday.

"I must check my schedule," I said. "I will have to let you know. I think it will be fine! But I will confirm on Monday."

He kissed me and pulled something out from his pocket—it was a gift for me!

A gift? Wow, that is really kind of him, I thought.

"Open it when you arrive upstairs and let me know if you like it!" he said.

We kissed in his car by my dorms. In my most elegant manner I thank him for the beautiful evening and walk away towards the steps of the main entrance.

In my room, I tear off the plastic paper and unpack the gift.

It was perfume, a brand called "Angel," in the shape of a star. There was also a card that said:

I had the feeling I was going on a date with an Angel. I was in the store and thought this would be the perfect fragrance for you, since it has your name on it!

Love,

Jason

I was a bit surprised, but very happy at the same time. I smoked my last cigarette and got ready for bed.

* * *

On Tuesday I was excitedly waiting to finish my shift. Jason has offered to get some take-out, then relax with him in his living room.

I placed my bullets with my gun and complete my handover; then I ran to my room for a shower to get ready for Jason.

He picked me up at 11am. The airbase was busy. One of my Italian co-workers saw me leaving the base with an American, and started spreading the news around! I did not really care. I was confident enough, and if they wanted to gossip about me, that was okay. They must have had a long, boring shift if the only thing they had to do was talk about me. I let them do it, as I wanted to focus on Jason, and had no time for distractions.

In the car with him everything felt so different—he made me feel safe and protected. I did not worry about anything; stress felt far away from me. The only thing we had to think about was what kind of takeaway to order.

"I could go for Italian," he said.

"I feel more like Chinese," I replied.

"Fine, let's get Chinese then!"

We got food and some drinks, then left for his house. When we arrived we started eating right away, since I was starving!

We sat in the dining room. He started telling me about his favourite meal, and I was very surprised at how he could eat a fresh hot pepper with his food while talking normally with me. I do love spicy food, but that pepper was too hot for me! I decided to try it; I spent ten minutes in the bathroom drinking milk and trying not to cry!

It was about 2pm in the afternoon. We were chilling in his living room, having just finished the meal. I offered to help him with the clean-up.

"No, darling, just relax and watch some TV," he said.

"Okay, then." I considered his use of the word 'relax.' I took off my shoes, and with the noise of the washing machine in the background and his footsteps in the kitchen while he was washing the dishes, I fall asleep.

When I woke up, I opened my eyes slowly. I stopped. Jason was sitting next to me, watching me while I slept. It was dark outside, and from the living room window I could see the stars.

"Jason?" I said. "What time is it?"

"It is 11pm darling," he replied. "Do you know you look beautiful when you sleep? So peaceful with your relaxed breathing."

I sat bolt upright. "Oh my God, Jason! I must go back to the base—it is so late!"

He shrugged. "You can stay here," he said.

I shook my head. "I am so sorry Jason, but I must get back to the base; an officer checks to see if we're all in our rooms every day around 11:30pm. Can we be there before 11:20?"

"Sure, get ready," he said gamely. "I will be waiting in the car for you!"

Another thing that I hated in the military. In addition to the morning anthem, you also needed to confirm your presence every day at 11:30 in the evening. If they noticed that you were not in your room, they could fire you, or at the very least drop your score from excellent to good. Of course, Jason was a very strong, almost irresistible temptation for me, but I also needed to follow base policy.

Therefore, as soon he stopped the car I kissed him and started running to the dorms. I was so lucky... the officer had just passed my colleague's room, ready to move on to mine. Luckily, I was there next to him right on time.

He asked me how my day was, and with an authentic smile I said, "I was very busy with the training; I want to pass the exam, so I was busy studying!"

"Studying English with that American, or studying for your career?" he asked. He looked me in the eye and said, "You are very special, and smart! When I was your age, I was in love with an American girl. But her contract expired, and she left me here; she had just used me. Don't be his distraction! If you just want to have fun, that's fine, but don't get into a serious relationship unless you want to be dumped when you are not expecting it."

I couldn't say even one word to all that, as I was aware that Jason's contract expired in two years' time, and he was planning to leave when that happened. But at the same time, I was really happy about our dating; he was always nice with me. Why should I stay single and alone?

I was here on my own as well, with no family, and surrounded by people that I didn't really care to socialise with. They were all so focussed on getting their work done, then going back to their rooms. I wanted to enjoy my time and my life there at Aviano Air Base and get to know the culture, the people, and the mountain. With Jason this was possible. He was, like me, interested in discovering new things and learning more about the future; to travel around and learn about something new all the time. Plus, he was cute, he made me feel happy and safe, and I was learning English with him—so why should I stop all this?

I love to live in the moment, and I was not planning on getting married. So I thought to myself, *Why not enjoy the military together with Jason?*

This time with Jason was very special to me. I am of the strong opinion that the best way to learn a language is to start a friendship with a native speaker. Jason was very patient with me, and with plenty of fun chats over drinks, I was speaking English better and better every day. I have to thank his consistent patience with me.

Jason was the first person to give me a good way to practice my English, and after a couple of weeks I was talking faster. Soon, I could have a conversation at Gate 9 with the Americans!

They were also were aware that I was dating one of their men, so they began to give me more peanut butter, and were even nicer to me than before.

Jason always corrected me when I was talking, improving my use of the language. It was a lot of effort on his part, but he would explain to me new synonyms and better ways to pronounce a word. So I have to say a very big "thank you" to him and my American co-workers!

I also noticed that once I started speaking English more fluently, Gate 9 was no longer on my list of placements. My team was very envious that I was working in the office: I was given the opportunity to translate American documents into Italian and ensure that all the data was up-to-date.

I was very pleased with my accomplishments, and for my relationship with Jason helping me to achieve my goals.

That beautiful period was one of many more to arrive.

Although I had many successes in my life before this, I had not felt complete. I needed to be next to a person like Jason.

After we were dating for about a month, he began asking me if I would like to spend a weekend with him. I decided to take two days off, so that I didn't have to rush back to the dorms to confirm my presence. Jason was always getting weekends off; therefore, I packed my suitcase to take the essentials I would need to spend a weekend away!

I was in a good mood. Jason picked me up and from Pordenone. From there we went to Slovenia to spend the night there. With him, I didn't worry too much about booking or confirmations, as he had thought of everything; he had already booked a hotel called the Landscape.

"Darling, are you okay?" he asked on the way.

"Never feeling better," I answered.

He reached a hand over to my side of the car, stroking me over my underwear while was driving. He unbuttoned his trousers and said, "It is only fifteen minutes' drive to the hotel, babe."

But we were too much in love to wait. We stopped the car in

an emergency space on the highway.

He started to touch me more fervently, and we moved to the back seat of the car. He runs a hand along my leg, licking my neck. My desire for him grows, and my fantasies were too grand to be satisfied here in the backseat.

He paused, then said, "I know what you want! Get out of the car, just keep your shoes."

On the empty side of the highway we could hear a wolf out in the forest, howling, the crickets everywhere, and then our moaning.

Normally, I wasn't easily satisfied—well, I was never satisfied, not the way I really wanted it. But Jason ... oh, that man, he could make me scream and moan over and over. It was as if he never had to stop, maybe because he worked out every day and led a healthy life—well, not too healthy, seeing as he drank every day!—but with him I could be satisfied.

We could see the hotel from the edge of the road. As soon as we had stored our luggage in the room, we could not stop kissing and kissing each other.

For me, I found it difficult to trust someone, especially after all my experiences in the past, but my ease with Jason was not just about trust! The feeling that came so naturally to me with him, after several relationships in Sicily before I joined the air force, was that for the first time I was feeling in love.

Because I let myself be loved by someone. I opened my heart without thinking about what came next: the future, a the family, a wedding, etc...

The most common mistake to make when we start dating is to become so worried about what comes next that we never focus on the moment. That moment! The moment that takes us away from negativity and stress.

Dear readers, it was my time! Finally, the time that I had been waiting for. To fall in love.

Love is dangerous; you can never fully understand the feeling, but you know that you are totally immersed in it when you cannot stop thinking about the other person: when you desire to kiss and hug them, when you know that they can read your mind without even speaking. Because love is magic: magic like a kiss, magic like a lovely cuddle, and you know that you are in love when you don't see any imperfections in your loving partner!

He was my champion, my best friend, my dad, my brother: he was there to support me and give me the motivation to achieve my goals; to be calm when I was nervous, to show care when I was busy with other things.

We sat there, holding each other's hands, and I thought to myself for the first time, What a wonderful world!

That night changed my opinions about men. I understood that even if you were heartbroken, or your ex-boyfriend did not deserve you because he was loser, it did not mean that all men were the same. There was always that opportunity waiting, and you just had to wait for your time: to be at the right place at the right time; it was possible, and just because it had not happened yet, it didn't mean that it would not happen.

Everyone has their weaknesses, and mine was impatience. I used to think I had everything I wanted to have: friends who were there for me anytime I called. They would always come running to me, not because I was Alexa, but because I was a boss involved in the Mafia; they were scared of the consequences if I was kept waiting too long.

I know, it is difficult to change as you grow older; therefore, you don't need to change but rather improve that part of you, that weakness. Try to find opportunities to make that part of yourself better. Work on it every day, and let your partner know about your dark side, so that they can give you some feedback and make you understand what you should work on and what you should not.

Jason was a big part of my life: with his love he made me forget about my dad and my past. Finally, I felt free. It was as if I had paid my price, knowing I could have my freedom after.

Yes, I was free, and I was in love.

That weekend away changed my opinions about people and love. I didn't regret one single moment I spent with Jason, because he was the one who cleared away the scar over my heart with his love. Until one day...

The day when his contract expired, and he had to return to

the States.

* * *

Jason began to act differently with me; he was very confused. He felt he had to go home, but we didn't want to separate. So we decided to see how things could work with us together in the States; I packed my luggage and flew over there with him.

New York was very different compared to Europe. Healthy food was overpriced, and rubbish food was very cheap. It was a very expensive city, especially if you drove to downtown. Monthly rent was about three thousand euros.

Anything and everything was possible there. There were so many different job offers. It was the city that never slept: the lights inspired me. New York was divided into five districts: Brooklyn, The Bronx, Queens, Manhattan, and Long Island. It was beautiful to live there, but as soon as I met Jason' family, there were a few conflicts.

I do love and respect Indian culture, but don't force me to do something that I am not keen to do. For instance, Jason' mother took me to the shopping mall, not to buy me a dress, but to buy me a sari.

When you are in love, you will do anything for that person. I did not realize at that time my Italian culture was being turned into an Indian one. I didn't understand why Indian people would leave India to raise a family in New York, but keep their strong traditions, just as though they were still in India; going to Indian restaurants, wearing a sari around Manhattan, socialising only with Indian friends and relatives. I believed if you are travelling around new countries and seeing new places, it is good to meet other cultures and share new experiences.

I am open-minded, and I absolutely love to try different types of food, but every single day we ate the same thing: basmati as the first course and chicken as the second, with some appetisers called Samosa and Pakora. The food was very spicy, but I did enjoy it.

Indian weddings are very nice, but the bride and groom never dance close to each other. And as long you cook and you look after the house, you are a perfect bride.

I wasn't there in New York to learn how to cook Chicken Biryani. I was there for Jason, for our love, and to find a job opportunity that could raise our love even higher. My plan was to stay happy with him and with a job.

But his mother was always in the way between us. I had tried to talk to her, but she was too narrow-minded to make her understand my thoughts. It hadn't been a good idea to move to New York; his mother tried to convince me to marry her son, so they organized an engagement party.

I spoke with Jason about that; how there was too much pressure on my shoulders. I felt that I was in an impossible position. So I decided to return to Italy.

I broke up the relationship with Jason. I had big hopes for us, but you cannot live your life on hopes alone.

* * *

A year later, I applied to join the Italian State Police, the Polizia di Stato; my experience in the Air Force was strongly taken into consideration. I had decided to think more about my life and my personal goals.

My application was successful, so I began to travel around Europe once again. Then, Jason called me. He wanted to re-join the Air Force and follow my destinations with his security job.

As we had been together for so much time, having spent about six years together, I could not refuse his offer. He came to Italy first; then, we tried to schedule our missions to match our destinations together.

Everything was back to normal, until he was called for a mission in Kabul, Afghanistan. He stayed there for about six months; how he survived that mission was a miracle. All his co-workers died in an explosion. He was injured, but he survived; when he was with me, he never wanted to talk about how.

Instead, he spent most of each day drinking Jack Daniels and watching TV. He would be drunk by 11am sometimes. I'd had enough. So, I decided to pay for a mental help therapist. According to the therapist, he had depression caused not just from the explosion, but because on that mission he had killed a four-year old child who was carrying bombs strapped to her stomach. He had never told me, and still refused to share his experiences.

Unfortunately, the situation got worse.

* * *

It had been a year since Jason last worked, and he drank every day. He refused my help; he didn't want to move on at all. I spent all the year supporting him financially. I did try to push him to find a job, and to visit the doctor once a week.

He started to use heroin as well. In a way, I understood; although I'd had a hard life, I had never killed a child. I understood the pain in his heart, but life needed to continue. I couldn't think about him as a fiancé anymore. His depression had consumed him for more than a year, and he could not get better. I tried to convince him to visit the psychiatrist again to focus on his mental health.

In the meantime, my period was late.

I was under a lot of stress because I was supporting both of us, working hard, working a double-shift every weekend to make enough money to support us and pay the therapist as well. I told myself that maybe that was the reason.

I argued with Jason often, as I was working crazy hard, but then he would waste our money on alcohol and drugs. I thought to take it easy with him, because otherwise I felt my life would fall into that dark tunnel of my Black Moon again.

My period still hadn't come. So after my morning jog, I bought a pregnancy test.

It was positive.

I wasn't ready to have a baby. Especially with a father who was a heroin addict and not as responsible as he was before.

That evening I showed him the pregnancy test results during dinner and told him the news. I could still change my mind and keep the baby, but he told me that he preferred to go back to New York and stay with his family.

Two weeks after I found out I was pregnant, a friend of mine who was a gynaecologist and knew my situation gave me three pills: very strong pills that would make me abort.

I realized after that episode that I had started to fall again into my Black Moon. I talked to the therapist myself, and she convinced me to accept that if our relationship was over, it was not my fault. She made me focus on my personal goals again, setting for me some new, strong challenges to keep my mind distracted from Jason.

I took a break from him, as I was trapped twenty-four hours a day with his depression. I had stopped talking with my family. I had stopped going out with friends. I had stopped smiling.

As soon I stepped away from Jason, I saw a life still going on outside: the world, the beauty of this earth. I came back to the house after a couple of days. That time away was important for me to think about my options and make the right choice.

I saw him on the sofa, as usual, finishing a bottle of Jack Daniels. "Hey, where have you been?" he said.

"I took some time to think," I replied. "Jason, listen. I am sorry if I am not strong enough to support you. What do you want to do with your life? What will make you happy?"

"I am happy with you," he said, gesturing with the bottle.

I shook my head. "Jason, you have changed so much. You have improved as well, but I think Europe is not good for you anymore; you deserve to be next to your family. Someone who will look after you every day, someone who can control you while you are weak during this time."

The next day, he stopped drinking. He booked a one-way ticket for NYC in a week's time.

On the day of his departure, I made some pasta for him to take with him on the plane. I dropped him off at the airport and tried to say a lot of positive words to make him feel good and proud of his decision. He stopped before the security gate and kissed me and hugged me for about five minutes; although he was a drug addict, he did truly love me the whole time.

As soon as he disappeared behind the security gate, I received a text from him:

Thanks for everything you did for me. I am on the plane, I will text you when I am in New York.

I replied:

Don't worry; I look forward to receiving your text. Have a safe trip.

That day was the last time I ever saw him.

Driving away from the airport, I had tears in my eyes thinking about our beautiful relationship together. Eight years together. He was my first love—and my last, as I did not find a person like him again.

I did not regret a single moment of my time with him.

Although we don't talk as we did before, he will always remain in my heart. I respect him, and I thank him for everything he did for me, the good and the bad. Not as a delusion, but as an important experience in my life that helped me to grow in a lot of aspects of my mind and the way I see things.

Jason now is an IT head manager, working in New York. He has his life back together again. This is what is important: that he is safe and happy with his career.

7. Money Laundering

I was involved in money laundering at a very young age.

Money laundering is a crime, as we all know, but for Giuseppe it could only be described as a "favour."

The term "laundering" is used because criminals turn "dirty" money into "clean" funds that can then be integrated into the legitimate economy as though they had been lawfully acquired. It is often a process that transforms a huge amount of criminal funds into clean, "legitimate" cash. One of the largest property investors once said that if money laundering were a company, it would probably be the 4th largest company in the world.

Malta is one of the most popular places for money laundering, followed by Switzerland and Iran. Unfortunately, in Sicily money laundering is very common, as Malta is right next door.

When I was with Giuseppe in Sicily, I knew his most common sources of criminal funds came from extortion, dodgy deals, prostitution, drug dealing, fraud, and firearm selling. I tried to understand how he cleaned that money, and I came to understand that this illegal activity is comprised of three distinct stages: placement, layering, and integration.

Placement is the first step of moving money that has been earned through crime away from its source. This can be as simple as putting the money into a bank account, or using it to buy assets, such as property or goods.

I would sometimes be asked the "favour" of moving the dirty money. Giuseppe would often ask me to go on down to the housing market and pick a property to buy. I liked this task, being able to pick out a nice villa, maybe even finding one with a private swimming pool. Giuseppe always made sure that the money I was sent to move included enough for a good tip for the agent and his silence.

The second step, layering, can get a bit delicate. This step is integral to hiding the origins of the dirty money. Numerous transactions must be made in order to "wash" the money, making it difficult to trace it back to criminal activity and thus appear clean.

There are many ways this can be accomplished: our most common way of doing so was buying gold or spending and exchanging it at a casino. Most Friday nights I would find myself at the casino with Giuseppe's team. Whatever winnings I didn't use we'd hold on to as a receipt, and at the end of the night resell them to get new cash back.

Reintegrating the money back into the economy is the last step. This is to make it look as if the money came from a legitimate source. For example, a "front" company can be used, submitting invoices that are then paid in cash, or requesting loans that are fulfilled with the laundered money.

The newly-clean cash now needs to be spent. How? Easy. Invest in property, buy an expensive car, buy some business shares, or invest in such a way that no one will notice.

So how do you know if you are involved in a money laundering situation?

The most common way one gets involved in this crime is by doing a monetary favour for a friend. For example, if a friend hands you some cash and asks you to transfer it into their bank account. You might not ask questions, because you believe them to be your friend and thus accept the request as genuine. But stop and think first about the amount of cash he is asking you to transfer into his account.

Think about where the money may have come from, and why they have asked you to transfer it into their account in the first place. You may be committing a financial crime, unaware of the consequences. Be especially wary if the amount exceeds the ten thousand euros, as this will inspire a police interrogation.

The only way to stop such financial crime is to identify the criminal activities and detect the source of the transactions, stopping corruption. Increase the check points: check points for everyone. If every individual were strong enough to refuse illegal activities in exchange for money, this could be a first step to stopping money laundering. If everyone were to act with morality and honesty, that would avoid corruption. Doing the right thing will save us all from fraud and financial crimes.

I once asked Giuseppe how he could have so many different avenues for laundering money and not being detected.

He calmly replied, "Alexa, remember that an economic crisis often damages businesses. Their owners will do anything to save them from bankruptcy. This is why people come to me. In exchange, it is an easy favour for us to ask an everyday business such as a coffee shop, street vendor, barber shop, club, or casino to clean dirty cash by transferring it between different bank accounts."

"But Toto, how can you clear away all the evidence of that?"

"Well, Alexa. It is difficult to get any evidence in the first place, because if you have the right connections and you don't have a criminal record, you look like a genuine person with a good reason to have all that money. Alexa, this is why you are just the right person to help me with this."

That day I started learning how to clean dirty funds.

The feeling was amazing. Especially when I had such huge amounts of cash around me. The first time that I saw such a huge amount of cash, I asked my friend to take a photo of me wearing my bikini; my body was covered with thousands of banknotes. My body was worth a fortune!

"Toto? Is this money only coming from criminal funding?" I once asked him.

"Well, Alexa, sometimes these favours are also from terrorist funding."

"How do you know, Toto?"

"My dear Alexa, you are too young for this subject." He tried to brush me off with a wave of his hand.

But I insisted. "How can I be too young if I am old enough to be helping you with it?"

Giuseppe sighed. "Very well. Money laundering and terrorist financing usually differ in how they obtained their money. With money laundering, the money is usually earned through criminal activity. This may be from a single person, such as with embezzlement, or it may be from large organization such as us. But the source in money laundering is always from … shall we say, 'illicit' activity."

"I see … but Toto, what about terrorist funding?"

"With terrorist financing, the money doesn't always come from less-than-legal activity; the initial source may be legitimate. It may be that they have a wealthy benefactor who agrees with the terrorists' goals and wants to support their activity. It may be from groups that pose as charitable organizations collecting donations but then, rather than use it for charity, they transfer the money to terrorist groups or operatives."

At my puzzled frown, he added, "That's not to say that the source of terrorist funds is never criminal in origin. Recently, more terrorist groups have engaged in criminal activity, such as ransom, blood diamonds, arms dealing, and human trafficking, to eliminate their reliance on donors and thus become self-supporting."

Giuseppe leaned back, drink in hand, really getting into the topic now. "Money laundering and terrorist financing also differ in the total amounts normally dealt with. When we clean money, the total amount is usually quite large." He gazed intently at me, to ensure I was paying attention. "This requires us to be both more careful and more creative in how we move the money. Generally, the total gets broken up into smaller amounts and then moved; this makes it look as natural as possible."

He smiled at me. "This is where you can help me, my dear Alexa. When you turn eighteen, I will arrange a passport for you to travel and help me as you expand your knowledge."

"How can we get the best result out of it, Toto?"

"Right now Alexa, don't get into much of this: just focus on a small amount. If you listen to my advice I promise you, you would be the richest person in Italy. It is these smaller amounts—and the original legitimacy of the funds—that require less creativity to move without triggering alerts."

He thought pensively for a minute. "You are very good at driving your scooter about for us. Perhaps I will get you a truck driving licence. Would you like that? Our couriers sometimes smuggle cash into other countries that have more relaxed detection systems. They can earn ten thousand euros for one easy job!"

"Really Toto? That's a lot of money for one job. But … I don't know if I want to be that involved. It sounds like corruption is both the key and heart of money laundering."

"Come on Alexa, don't be silly; couriers take many different circumstances to be identified, and we are better than that. I will make sure that you will be an ambulance driver. You would not suspect that an ambulance on duty might be one of the links in the chain of a financial crime."

He leaned forward, a twinkle in his eye. "So Alexa, when do you want to start?"

"…Okay Toto, I will be think about it and let you know."

8. My Dad's Return

After eight years of a fantastically-close relationship with Jason, my single life was very different: the bed was huge, the shower was always clean, the house looked organized all the time, and the smell was as fresh as flowers picked that day.

My next-door neighbour had noticed that I was returning home alone every night. He invited me to dinner, but I was not in the mood to be around people.

Friends came back into my day-to-day life, and after six months my life was back to normal. I still thought about Jason, but not like before: it was in a positive way, this time. To stay strong, I kept following my routine and healthy lifestyle. In order to keep my mind busy, I joined a boxing class, studied business, played tennis during the weekend, and had dinner and nights out with friends at the club.

My contract with the Polizia di Stato was set to change, too. When I saw Sicily on my mission program for the next year, I went to my officer and asked why.

He only said, "Never try to escape from your problems! Identify them, confront them, and then you can forget them. Sicily is your place, Alexa; you should be happy to be there near your family."

"Officer, could I go to Kosovo or Iraq instead?" I smiled and tried to convince him. But there was nothing I could do to change his mind.

Therefore, after some camomile tea and a few glasses of wine, I decided to sign the contract.

A week later, I flew from Germany to Rome, then from Rome to Catania. My mom was waiting for me at the airport with flowers, and my grandparents were at the house, ready to have a family lunch.

All my old memories back, those I could not erase from my mind, came rushing back; the smell of the Mediterranean Sea reminded me of when I was young, driving my scooter around, hanging out with Chiara and my friends. The negative memories, too, hit my mind like a lightning strike. It was difficult to be in the place that I hated the most and loved the most; it was an interminable, unwinnable battle with myself. Like going one-on-one, with no one able to come out the winner.

That afternoon, I called Chiara and told her that I was in Sicily for about one year. Since I had left, I'd kept Chiara's details and used different mobile phones to contact her, just for safety reasons; I did the same with my family.

Upon arriving at my mother's house, I went up to my old room. On my bed, there were a large number of letters. Then I hear my mother's voice, "Lexi! Those letters are for you, love; I didn't open them because they have your name on it."

"Thanks, Mum," I said.

My luggage was waiting to be unpacked, but I was curious to open those letters first. Most of them were bills, advertisements, and bank statements.

Suddenly, I noticed that a few of them were from prison. Giuseppe had written me a letter, and written recently as well, which was a surprise!

His words spoke to me from that crisp, white paper:

Dear Alexa,

I am sorry about everything; I asked too much of you. All those things you did for me, I didn't understand when I was hurting you, because I was too busy with other things. You never refused to help me with your smile, your energy, and your love.

I miss your positivity; I will pay a fortune just to see you once again.

As you know, the judge gave me twenty years. But I don't know if I can stay here without you; I would rather die. I need you. Please, if you see this letter, come to visit me.

Love,

Giuseppe

For a moment, I had the acute sensation of being stabbed in the back. I hadn't even known that he was in prison: it was all a shock to me.

Then, there was a second letter from prison, this one from someone else:

Dear Alexa,

We have done a lot of things together. I am writing to thank you for everything you did for me, for every time you stayed quiet and defended me. I never forgot your kindness or your smile.

I am here again, this time for about ten years.

Stay safe,

Mario

Mario had been my boyfriend back in Sicily. We used to sell firearms together; while he was with me, I had to save his ass many times: he used to put his gun on the top of the car and then drive off without it. Several times I told the big boss that it was my fault, tired as I was because of my school hours.

Wow, this is a cold shower. Chiara had been right about the end of this cycle.

I took a break from those letters, then went to the kitchen and spent time with my mom and our cat. While we were there, the doorbell rang.

"Hello? Who is it?" I called.

"Lexi! It is me, Chiara!"

"Chiara?"

Chiara walked in with a child holding her hand. "Alexa! Oh my God, it has been such a long time." She hugged me tight. "You are so beautiful," she added.

I was at a loss for words. Chiara laughed. "Well, I did say I have a surprise for you!" She pointed her finger to the child. "This is the surprise. Matteo? Say 'hi' to Auntie Alexa."

"Matteo, you look so cute," I said. "How old are you?"

"I am five years old!" he said, puffing up his chest proudly.

"Wow, you are a Superman now!" I added.

Chiara told me about Matteo's father. Apparently he was a

bad guy: a loser, an alcoholic, and she was divorcing him.

"Alexa, it is okay, that happens; that's life," she said. "But listen, I am not here only for that ... there is something that you need to know. It is about your father."

"My father?"

"Yes, Alexa: your dad is back in the city. I saw him once at the store wearing sunglasses and a hat; he looked like he didn't want to be recognized. He is hiding something, and you are the best person to find out what. You can use your official ID to follow him, or maybe just watch outside his door..."

I didn't hear what else she said. My legs were shaking; it had been a long time since that had happened. I paused to think, then said, "Well Chiara, I have a life now, and I am out of it; I don't want to go back in that game."

She insisted, "Alexa, it is your dad—he is still your dad, you should see him and meet him! I know it is hard, as he left you in 2003, but now you are a strong, independent woman, no longer his little girl. You can just meet him for coffee, nothing more. I think he will be very happy to see you."

"Mum?" I called to her in the other room. "Mum?"

"Yes, love."

"Mum, did you know that Dad is back here again?"

She nodded sombrely. "Yes, honey I knew that; I did not say anything right away, as I didn't want to upset you."

I was feeling very agitated. Everyone had known that my father was back in the city ... and nobody had called to tell me about it. Crazy!

I found out where my dad now lived. Then I decided to be the "man" of the situation, and be the one to reach out to him. I considered that maybe he was scared to have the family discover that he was back in town.

I was driving an Alfa Romeo MiTo at that time, black and manual. I enjoyed the feeling of smoking a cigarette and playing good music while feeling connected to its speed. I turned off the car and waited in the parking lot where, according to Chiara, my dad lived.

His car was parked there, so I sat back in my car. I read a book, had a latté, and then, a few hours later, he was there.

He had walked up, and was heading for the front door while pulling out his keys. He looked much the same as he had when he'd left that day, thirteen years ago. I still remembered that day clearly: just like a CD that loops back to the start, it was the kind of memory that can never be replaced or erased from your mind. It was permanent.

In that moment, my emotions overwhelmed me, making it too difficult to stay calm. My first thought was to get out of my car, slap him in the face, and push him to the ground, then tell him just how much he had hurt me over these many years. That was the devil on my shoulder talking. My angel tried to pull me in the opposite direction, telling me that he was still my father, and that contact and explanation could bring forgiveness. What if I could forgive, heal all my scars, and turn that damage into a positive experience?

My mind was fighting, these two sides of me pitted against each other: one being anger and madness, the other peace and forgiveness. How could I find a balance? In the face of it all, I couldn't even get out of the car.

I saw him shaking hands with another guy while he walked into the apartments. I had missed the chance to speak to my father, but I did follow the other guy to see what he did. He went to a pharmacy, then, stood around outside, obviously waiting for someone. I waited too.

A familiar-looking man approached him. Where did I know this guy from? I tried to remember, thinking back through my past life. Yes, I knew him: he was Giuseppe's brother.

Was that a coincidence, or was something bad going on?

If my father had been kidnapped, ran away, or whatever it was to cause him to disappear for so long, it was always because of Giuseppe and his boys; so why now are they connecting with my dad? It was something that I couldn't understand.

I didn't want to talk with that man about it; I preferred to wait to hear what my dad had to say about it.

It was late evening by then. I drove by my uncle's shop: my father's brother was there. I leaned out the window and said, "Hi!" to him from the car.

He saw me, puzzled at first, then he met my eyes. "Alexa? Oh my God, you are so pretty!" he said. "Where have you been, it has been such a long time! Would you like a coffee?" he added with his fake smile.

I could never forget my dad's family. They were so attached to money and their business; they never considered my mother, who had been left alone to raise me by herself. They had never tried to provide her with any kind of support, morally or financially. They were so cold in their hearts, those kind of rich people who have only envy for a sincere person like my mom.

They were aware of my dad's departure. I was not aware of anything about them; the only thing they did during all those dramatic years was force me to sign for every note I received from them. They would then take a photo of me with those notes in my hands as evidence that I was satisfied with their money. I was too young to understand what was in their minds.

Now everything came back to me, a natural confirmation that what I had assumed was not wrong: these people were not my family. I hope that their blood is not shared in my body, because I have never met such stingy people in my life. The kind of people who prefer money over helping a child, making every excuse just to run their business; the more money they earned, the more they wanted.

My father's mother used to give me money in the cradle, sliding it under the mattress when I was about two years old. My mom was disappointed by this, as my grandmother would also pray while placing the money, as if she were practicing some superstitious way to make me addicted to materialism.

I drank my coffee, than asked about my Dad. "So, I heard Dad is in town? Where does he live?"

I knew where he was living, I just asked the question to see what my uncle would tell me.

"Yes, Alexa, he is around," he said. "He is living in your uncle's flat, the one opposite the Piazza."

Of course, I know where he was. But I pretended it was news. "Cool. May I please have his number, so I will able to call him?"

"Sure, Alexa, but maybe it would be better if I asked him first?"

His voice was amicable, but his smile was tight.

"You really want to ask my father if he would allow you to give his number to his own daughter? You seem cold, Uncle, is everything all right with you?" I added.

My uncle fiddled with his coffee cup. "It is not that, Alexa. I really do care about you, I just do not want to get caught in the middle of anything."

I really felt like there was something bad going on now, and I had to try to control my emotions. When I had a handle on them, I said, "Hey Uncle, don't worry; I will not put you in the middle of anything. You are not going to be involved, I can guarantee it. Now, can I please have that number?"

As soon as I got what I wanted, I gave him a stiff hug, then walked back to my car.

Finally, I could get in touch with the man who had damaged my life and arrange to meet him face-to-face.

I took the elevator, and pressed floor number four to reach my flat, hiding that piece of paper with his number in my jeans packet as though it were my first date.

I spoke with my mom before calling him. She thought the best idea would be to meet him with a lawyer, or even a guard present, because after all these years nobody knew what his intentions were.

I didn't want to put my lawyer in the middle of this—I just wanted to have a one-on-one with Dad. Therefore, I summoned up some courage and dialled his number.

The phone rang. Then, "Hello? Who is this?"

"Dad? It's me?" My heart stopped, and for a moment, nothing was going through my mind.

When he finally responded, his voice sounded scared. "Lexi! My love, where are you?"

"I am in town! Can we meet? I have a car; I can pick you up."

"Yes!" he said. "Come by the Piazza. I will get ready and wait for you there."

I decided to wear a dress and put on makeup, to ensure I looked my best. So he could regret all those years he left me for ... I wanted to make sure that he understood what he had missed by looking at every part of my outfit!"

I drove towards the Piazza and parked my car. I saw him walking, and headed toward him. After all those years, the word "Dad" could not come to my mouth very easily. "Hi D-Da-Dad. Sorry, Dad, it's just been such a long time of not saying that word, I cannot really say it anymore ... How are you? How have you been?"

He tried to hug me, but I was shaking, with so many emotions whirling inside me that I forgot what I supposed to say. Like when you study so hard for a test, and then when in front your teacher you forget the answer. Or a singer who practises every day at home, but as soon he steps on stage, he gets shy and stops. It was like I was stuck in space and time.

I tell myself firmly, *Come on Alexa, you can do this*. Then the light returns, and my voice is suddenly back. "Dad, you hurt me; you made me a piece of shit; you destroyed my life that day you left me at school without saying a word. I was in the hospital when I crashed my scooter, and where were you? Where were you when I had my first boyfriend, when I had my eighteenth birthday party, my communion in church ... you missed everything, Dad!"

I took a deep, shaky breath. "You missed thirteen years of my life. I preferred to think you were dead instead of disappearing like a ghost: where are your balls? I looked for you everywhere; you left Mum by herself without money or support. I mean, really Dad? I thought you were clever!"

He stepped back, blinking, but I steamrolled on. "Dad, you made me close off my heart to everyone, leaving me aggressive and unable to trust anyone. Every Christmas I used to pray to God for your return, asking Santa Claus to bring me a Dad instead of a present! You missed a lot, and trust me, that time can never come back."

I realized that my voice was raised, but at that point I didn't really care. "And to top it all off, you made my pay your council tax for about ten years, plus all the bills and debts you owed people around town. You owe me more than fourteen thousand euros, which I wasted on your debts. I could pay for my Master's with that money! Do you really understand what this means?"

I stopped my negative tirade to take a break. I reminded myself that I was sitting in a public area by the Piazza, and that I was here to try to listen him as well.

He was very quiet for a time. Then he said, "Lexi! You've said you were damaged, you were hurt: that you had scars on your body. But you look fine; I don't see any of those bloody scars that you have mentioned!"

Suddenly, I thought about my mother, who had warned me about my dad's mental state. This man was not my father anymore! He was acting like a lone wolf, maybe because he'd had too much time by himself and couldn't reach home as he'd wanted. But that shouldn't matter, because a father should still do anything for his child.

He was happy to see me, of course, but I didn't expect the words that he said. I thought he was there to hug me and get our relationship back. I was ready to forgive him. After that day, I decided to give him another chance.

I was stupid; I did not realize that my dad was not acting like a father anymore. What was his role now? What mask was he wearing? Why was he cold to me? Why was he meeting with a friend in touch with Giuseppe's brother?

I felt those knives stabbing me in the back again. He was not going to help me with my scars, because he was just some guy to me now, even if I was born from his sperm. But he was not my blood anymore, he was another person.

I was considering spending more time with him so I could try to understand—until I saw a letter on my doorstep from a legal advisor, which read:

Dear Ms. Ferilli,

I am writing to you to suggest selling your house.

According to a financial investigation, you live a comfortable life, drive an expensive car, and have a good career. It would be appropriate to put your home on the market, as your father owns a 50% share of this property. I strongly advise this, as he is struggling with money, and could potentially be under a financial depression soon. Selling the property will benefit your father's income and personal life.

I look forward to hearing from you.

Yours sincerely,

Legal Team

My hands were shaking when I read that letter! I could not believe who that guy really was anymore: a devil, an enemy— wherever he was, everything he touched was immediately broken and demolished.

I was so emotional that I decided to contact him.

"Hello?" he answered the phone.

"Hi, Dad, or whichever entity is inhabiting your body. Why did you send a legal letter?"

"I thought you would be happy to continue our relationship," he replied.

"I don't know who you are anymore," I spat.

"Lexi, I am sorry I cannot talk! Please call the lawyer if you want to get in touch with me. Have a good day!" He hung up.

Idiot! I was an idiot, but I could not regret anything. He was crazy for sure, but I was ready to forgive him, which meant, I needed to put that energy to forgetting about all the problems that he'd given me.

I also spoke with a police officer about my father. It turns out, Giuseppe was involved in my dad's kidnapping. Only my father was not truly kidnapped: he had escaped from Giuseppe.

Apparently, they used to work together. Then when the Euro caused the financial crisis, they decided to open a business together. My father did not recognize Giuseppe's share in the business, even though he was giving my father more than the 50% of the capital.

My father apparently called me to ask me to do all those things because he knew I was the only person that still believed in him; that was why when I had those phone calls, he never mentioned where he was, just told me that he was coming soon, but he never did.

The police officer confirmed that he only saw my father in town after Giuseppe was arrested. Because if Giuseppe had known that my father was in town, he would have done something bad to him.

Giuseppe hated my father; he had never told me that.

My father was in contact with Giuseppe's brother because he

was asking for more money for that old business, pretending to be a victim of failure; however, the business didn't exist anymore, since he never paid for anything and thus the business closed down when he left. My father was ruined, and he had run away with Giuseppe's money.

Now he was desperate, with no money: the only solution was to sell the house where my mother and I were living. Although I was tempted, I would never do such a cold thing to my mother. The share was half in my name, so I had the power to get back to his lawyer with a legal advisor to confirm that I was paying all his bills and had never received any financial support from him.

I was in the middle of a battle between Giuseppe, a criminal boss, and my father, a total liar.

I thought my father had been kidnapped. He was never kidnapped. Everything had been planned by the two of them, so nobody could understand what was going on.

Giuseppe used me against my father, making me do all those bad things just because I was his daughter. And my dad was the one who first mentioned my name to Giuseppe, telling him that I could help him out with those things in his place!

According to my lawyer and their investigation team, my father was in debt for over two million euros. Giuseppe had tried to help him, but asked to have his name in the business. My father refused unless Giuseppe gave him more money for that name; but as soon as my father got his money, he ran off, leaving my uncle to close the business a month later due to a fake economic crisis.

Who was the criminal then? My father, or Giuseppe?

I decided to go to my father's house for the last time.

I rang his doorbell. I was trying to be nice, but it was all fake—an act. I had my plan.

I was outside his house, but nobody seemed to be there. "Dad, can I come in?" I called. "I need to talk with you. I want to get our relationship back; please let me in!"

Suddenly there was a noise: he had buzzed me in. I went upstairs to his flat. As soon as I saw his face, I pushed him against the wall. I took a chair and hit it over his head, then pushed him up against the wall again. I was shouting at him, blaming him for everything he had done to me over the past thirteen years.

I heard a baby crying. He was not alone in the house.

Two young boys were yelling at me, "Stop, please! Leave Daddy alone! Don't hurt Daddy, please!"

Those voices stopped me from committing murder.

I had two brothers; he had never told me that I had siblings. But I didn't care anymore. I walked away from the flat, leaving him on the floor, alive.

I won the other 50% of the property after a six-month legal battle.

My father was happy with another family now. I was happy to be without a Father in my life; my brothers needed more support than I do. Unfortunately, his negative energy has been a strong influence in my life, and I needed to protect my own mental health.

Everyone has the right to choose what they prefer to keep in their lives. Unfortunately, you cannot choose your parents. But you can choose your happiness. Therefore, once my contract had nearly ended, I decided to visit him and properly meet my brothers.

I told him, that despite all the arguments we'd had in the past, I was ready to forgive him.

Which is what I did; not because he deserved it, but because it was the right thing to do to keep myself clear and honest. I didn't want to live a guilty life.

He shook my hand afterward, saying, "See you soon!"

"See you soon, Dad."

A "see you soon" is better than a "goodbye!" I walked away feeling stronger than ever; not because I had won against my father, but because my actions made me different from my father.

9. Her 30s Shades of Grey

Being the most respected girl in the neighbourhood was a great feeling. When I walked into a bar, someone would always welcome me with a warm smile, ready to offer me a drink and something to eat. When I went to the supermarket, the owners gave me extra items free of charge. At school, I would get free books for the year. I never paid the monthly subscription to use the gym, either, and I never paid the cover fee to get into clubs. Friends used to call me every day to invite me to bake cakes or cookies at their house, to go horseback riding, and many other activities. My life was very rewarding at that time!

But I wasn't showing myself; I was wearing a mask. Why? Because that mask helped me to be respected. Behind that theatre full of actresses, dancers, and artists, you would find the real me once the theatre's curtains close.

It was my dark side. That side was a mystery: hard to discover, hard to recover from, and hard to change. I hurt many people because I was not ready to change; letting that part go away was too difficult; or maybe I was so good at wearing a mask that no one could see my real personality.

Before Jason, I didn't believe in the love; the trauma my dad left me with made it too hard to ever trust another man. I never saw myself settling down with a guy; it was impossible to have that picture in my mind.

Therefore, anytime I was having sex, it was simply a biological exercise for me. I never slept with a guy again after a one-night stand. I used to smoke a cigarette with them. That was the only time that I gave to a man after having sex: three, maybe four minutes until I was finished my cigarette. Then I would get ready and walk away. Never looking back.

I did try to enjoy sex, but my fantasies were far from what I thought were normal for couples.

I discovered orgasms when I was young, too young. I used to play with myself when my school mates used to play with their dolls. One day, I was alone at home. My friends came over to do some homework for a school project. We decided to watch the Titanic, but inside the VHS machine, there was a pornographic movie.

I felt guilty, because when I looked into their innocent eyes, I saw true purity. For about a month afterward, they thanked me so much for that day, as they never talked about sex with their parents. No one had ever mentioned how it worked or all those forbidden mysteries related to the subject. I used to buy a pack of condoms and show them how to use them, in case they wanted to lose their virginity and avoid any unwanted surprises.

I lost my virginity when I was fourteen years old. The lucky guy came to my high school; not to take classes, but to sell weed.

One day, I met his eyes and he smiled at me. Then he turned his scooter and rode towards me. "Hi, I am Tony." He stood, holding his hand out in front of me. I stopped, gazing at him, losing myself in those brown eyes. I returned the handshake, then asked him why he had a scar on his hand.

"Oh, this? It was just from my pet," he responded.

That was hard to believe; it looked more like a knife scar. "I am Alexa, by the way," I said.

"Are you looking for some weed?" he offered. "I also have some cocaine. Try some, it's free for you; you will love it."

"Tony, thanks for your offer," I said, "But I don't smoke weed, I don't use cocaine, and I don't drink either." I had never been attracted to drugs. However, I used to drink some wine with my family; my grandfather had a vineyard that produced wine. I used to drink one glass of that wine at every Sunday lunch and feel very sleepy afterwards.

I gazed at him, then said, "I just think you can do better than that, you should study!"

He looked at me up and down with his eyes, silent. Then he left.

A short while later, on a summer day, I was walking home

from school. I heard someone called my name.

"Alexa! Alexa!" Followed by the noise of a scooter. Tony was riding it.

"Hi Tony, good to see you," I said. "What are you up to?"

"Fancy of a ride around the coast?" he asked.

I checked the time. "Only if you could take me home in one hour!"

"Of course," he assured me.

The air was fresh, and my hair whipped across my face from where it escaped the helmet. Just the two of us on a scooter surrounded by the landscape of the Mediterranean. Tony took my hand and placed it on his belly. My legs were shaking, and butterflies fluttered in my stomach. The crisp smell of salt filled my nostrils, giving me a sensation of freshness. All the while, he held my hand so tightly. I could feel his chest.

Then, he stopped the scooter in the middle of the street. "I forgot something..." Tenderly, he placed his hands over my cheeks, then kissed me.

I cannot remember exactly how long it lasted, maybe thirty seconds? But I remember it felt like a long, never-ending kiss.

That was the first of our many days together.

Tony was my first boyfriend. He was tall, and his skin was quite dark, with black hair and flat, brown eyes. He had a beauty spot on his right cheek, that looked good, a bit sexy, on his face. He would often wear a denim jacket and Timberland shoes; he had a tattoo on his neck that went up to his left ear.

Whenever I planned a date with Tony, I had to lie to my mother and hide from my friends, because I knew they would not approve. He had a bad reputation around the city: a twenty-one-year-old boy with four years behind bars, but with me he was the sweetest guy.

It was a bank holiday weekend, and mom was working. I went over to his house, and immediately he made me feel comfortable. He ran a bath for me. He lit candles, and handed me a glass of wine. Then he began to wash my back, again and again with the sponge, crossing his legs over mine. He licked my breast and touched it with the sponge; then he was touching me all over my body.

With those wide eyes I could get lost in, he asked, "Would you like to make love with me?"

I think for about few seconds. "Yes!"

He took a towel, putting it over my back. Then he kissed my shoulder and said, "I will wait for you in the bedroom."

Unfortunately, it was not good as I had hoped for in my dreams and fantasies.

It was my decision to stay with Tony in his house; I took a risk to see what he was really like. Where it could lead.

That wasn't love as I expected it to be.

He started to remove my towel, waiting until I was lying on the bed. I was feeling different: my arms waved in the air, and my vision blurred. While I was still very dizzy, I looked at him, telling him that I was not well.

But he continued kissing me, saying, "Relax, it is just you and me here. Don't think about anything."

The room spun around me. In the meantime, he took a rope and started to tie my ankles to the furniture, then he handcuffed me over the back of his bed.

I knew then that he had drugged me. He had added ecstasy in my drink; the last thing that I remember was his look when he took off his boxer shorts.

When I woke up, I found blood over his bed sheet: my blood. He had gone. I got dressed and ran away.

I had been raped. I had lost my virginity to a monster.

In my sweet innocence, I had considered Tony to be a perfect gentleman, but I was wrong. Boy, was I wrong!

A few months later, I saw a newspaper with his picture in it, saying that he had been arrested: they had found heroin and morphine in his house.

I was happy about that, because I then had my revenge.

I never said a word to my friends or my mom about him, because nobody was aware that I was seeing such a horrible person.

With that bad experience behind me, I started dating regular guys, of course. I did have a lovely boyfriend who treated me very well; he never let me down, but I just had my shades: my need. I lived with it, although it was not my fault.

When you have had a traumatic experience, if it is not carefully treated over time with love, attention, or therapy, it can affect your entire future, leading to sadness and negativity for the rest of your life.

I ran away from serious relationships, and I guess that made me hurt most of my boyfriends by being selfish and difficult to love. I used most of them to satisfy my own fantasies, then threw them away like objects. Binned like scrap paper: items that have served their purpose, my purpose. To use them instead of being used by them.

As soon I was satiated, I did not care too much about them. My sexual pleasure was made from, and now resided in, tortures. Cuddling, kissing, massages, watching romantic movies, gentle sex: I did not like any of that.

After the trauma with Tony, I dated a lovely guy. When I told him about my experience, he tried to make me very comfortable with my sexual life.

After that, I found myself again. As my pleasure, I added the addiction of adrenaline. It was like when I drove a motorbike and went really fast: although I knew it was dangerous, it was that speed that gave me a feeling of freedom, energy, and even relaxation— the feeling of being fully alive. It was hard to believe that I could fall asleep going those speeds, especially when my partner was driving. I would be in the back seat, and he would reach 220Km/h. He thought I would be scared; not at all, as I was sleeping at that speed. The emotion can be hard to describe: to put yourself in a situation that you enjoy, but on the other hand, you're crazily risking your life.

Sex was like that for me.

I never got tired of it, especially when I was the one who took the initiative. I didn't like to be kissed or hugged during it, and if I didn't have control of it, I didn't enjoy it so much. My common sexual fantasy was forcing a man to satisfy my perversions.

I also had few guys who lost their virginity with me. One of them was hurting so much that he cried; but I did not care that he was hurting, because he had agreed to have extreme sex with me.

When I wanted to have some fun, I would take a guy to a hotel, or go to Chiara's garage, depending on what I had in mind. I forced them to take me from behind, and to make me moan in an extreme way; if it was not painful, I did not reach orgasm.

If the guy was too soft, I told him to leave the hotel or the house. If they saw me walking in the street, they would stop me, begging for another chance. I was their drug; they couldn't understand that they were victims of my shades, my deep desires. They were addicted to me and my perversion, and the more they stayed with me, the more they couldn't run away to another girl. Just one meeting with me was enough for make them feel excited, happy.

It's crazy to think about it.

When I didn't care, they chased me. People want what they can't have. When I showed them my love, they hurt me or disappeared for no reason.

Therefore, I was not engaged. When they proposed or asked me to have a relationship, I would just thank them for the nice time, the lovely experience together, and tell them it was over. Because what I really wanted wasn't them.

I am a woman, and as you all must know by now, all women are complicated. My sexuality was more complicated than most. I also tried sex with another woman, but it did not work; I didn't deserve to be loved in that way.

Maybe I was influenced by Tony, or maybe I was looking for a substitute father. Or was I too weak to move on and find my own happiness?

I decided to talk with a therapist about it. She told me to just focus on myself.

I understood that, but what part of myself? The one that was destroyed, or the one that was weak? I could not truly express my opinion to her. She prescribed some strong sedatives to make me feel relaxed and sleepy, but that did not fix the problem. She was not good enough to make me face up to the truth.

All my traumas, and all the things that my eyes had seen, were stored in my mind, keeping me cold and insensitive. Was there a medicine that could make me forget about everything? Forget, and yet not destroy the weak part of myself.

The only medicine was the love.

But even that didn't happen overnight. It took a lot of time. This is especially true when you have a lot of delusions in your life, as I did; it can lead to a strong negative reaction. From my life experience, I strongly believe that achieving happiness is all about your reaction to events and how you take them.

There are different types of reactions to have in life: one is to fall; the other is to improve your skills. Sink or swim. The first is usually the most common. They say what doesn't break you, makes you stronger.

For example, if you are heartbroken, or your family is going through a divorce.

The most common reaction is to attempt to replace that feeling with another feeling: for example, to find another sexual partner or to get drunk with one's superficial friends, not the true friends who are there for you to give good advice. Instead you'll go out to just have fun clubbing, leaving everything behind whiling drinking, partying and getting high, waiting for that time when you feel better and can let that negativity leave you.

Many people react in different ways, but most people have the first reaction. On the flipside, there are few people, called smart people, that are clever enough to understand what kind of reaction will speed up their recovery time, leaving that messy and uncomfortable time in the past, and which reaction will accelerate that dark side.

But how? You have to think about how to react.

You could be heartbroken, your friends dumped you for another guy, your family could be going through a divorce, you've lost your job, or even just someone promised to take you out for dinner during the weekend, but they never did. Whatever it is, you are having a sad time, and this kind of negative feeling affects your day, your week, and your time.

This is how I have learned to control my 30 years of shades of grey: to ensure the light always came before the dark side. To protect myself against my delusions, and ensured they left my mind and my heart. I learned to stop and think: to pause first, and think about the negative feelings. Then I would change the word into "experience," and think about it from a positive perspective. That way, I could learn from those negative delusions, to learn from the experience; that was the key.

If you think that those bad memories are also experiences to help you grow, would you still be upset about them?

Because it is those experiences that have helped you to understand who you really are, not how the people want you to be or what they like about you. Because you are not those people: you are you.

We lost ourselves in technology, dealing with busy agendas, leaving our lives behind to focus on other lives.

Stop wearing that mask and look yourself in the mirror. Is that face familiar to you? Is that the real you?

Or is that you hiding behind a mask!

Every person is unique. But only a small percent of people can really understand my words. It is hard, I know, but not impossible. If you are confident and you believe in yourself, it is very easy to get into the right street.

Focus!

Easy to say ... but how? How did I learn to believe in myself? I paused and thought. I started with the people who loved me: my family, my friends, my pet. Then myself: I thought about me and my needs. I realized I needed to put myself first, then other people; that being a bit selfish was not wrong. I also had to believe in my own skills, in setting those goals that I had for myself. I made a list of my achievements and what I really wanted to do next.

Then I thought about those negative experiences. I lived with them every day to understand that they were only experiences in my life that made me better for next time. They helped me to see that wider vision, to see that it made me the person I am now.

Because if I were to dwell on those negative events and constantly cry over them, they would be there forever; but didn't want that: I wanted to be successful and happy, so I let them go in a positive way. Because I was an adult now, and consciously trying to live a good life, and it was all only because I had had those experiences in my life.

I was still made of the same stuff as I was before, but my way of seeing things had changed. I took responsibility, and understood that those feelings were only because I was going through a hard section of my life. But even that was something I could be happy about, because it meant my life was not that normal, was not that boring.

Those zigzag lines crossing my life made my journey interesting, and I am proud of them!

We all have scars from life. I was supported by different mentors, I was loved by different men, and I was helped by different friends and teachers who offered one-on-one support. My mother was also very important in my life. I had different therapists helping me to understand that it was not my fault.

It was, I think, not because I wanted to feel guilty. It was my fault because I could not accelerate the recovery process. I felt that if I had understood how to react from the beginning, maybe I would not have wasted all that time sitting on my sofa eating ice cream. I was lazy; or maybe, I did not want to react because I feared the chance.

After that long, dark tunnel I called Black Moon, finally ... I saw the change: the light! The magic, the love, the sunshine, and the positivity of living my life again. It wasn't about Jason, or about the love that he gave me, but of course that helped me out.

It was because I understood how to love myself more: how to look after me. How to conduct a healthy life, practise meditation, learn something new, stay away from drugs and alcohol, although not from the club, as I did love dancing. I learned that you do not fall if you are an open book, you fall if you keep yourself isolated from the world.

My depression was caused because I never took it to seriously. I used to hide myself from the people who loved me the most. I was sick and tired of being isolated. Dealing with crime made me grow, because I noticed that I was not like them: I was better than them.

Being aware that I had different parts of me, parts that were as different as the sun and the moon, the day, and the night. One part of myself was fine, the other part was destroyed—but that did not mean it was not there. It was only damaged.

It took time to get all those little pieces back together. But once I took them and put them back, it was so rewarding. I could finally look at myself in a different way. The face I saw in the mirror was my own.

I realized, it was this tension that was making me feel nervous.

People are too busy to look after you and take care of you. But you? You can do it! You are the only one who has that power—nobody can help you with that!

Once I realized that, I understood that if I could now achieve my goals and feel happy, it was only because I was ready to change.

The beginning was tough. There were times that I thought, Is now the right time to do it? The right time to change?

I had so many chances to implement that strength, to transform my weakness into a strength, and apply that strength into opportunity and challenges. Because only I could benefit from that change. My mental health needed to come first. The rest came later.

Everyone's lives are different, and my life was very tough and difficult to explain: difficult to let it go. Going from crime to serving the government was not easy. There were two distinct sides to my life. The illegal and the legal together: the illicit firearms and practise with those guns providing the training I needed to help me against bad people, to help protect the world.

If we can support each other more, at work, within our families, at being good people, at being good friends, I believe it could lead to a better world. We should enjoy the simplicity of this life. If you see something that doesn't look right, tell a friend, ask for their opinion, spread that voice: because that is the only way to stop corruption. I have learned that if you face a bad person, and what they are doing isn't right, you shouldn't just walk away: you should stop that person and make them understand why it is wrong. Teaching ethics and morality around the world is a must for everyone on Earth.

Spread the smile, not the negativity. Spread that love! Love does not cost a thing. I thank everyone who made me the woman that I am now. Because those experiences made me strong, made me the real me. The lady that I am now.

They made me, not a good person, but a better person...

10. Unchained

Have you ever thought about leaving for good?

I have.

It was 7:30 in the morning, and I was about to check in with Alitalia Airline. Destination: Gatwick Airport, London.

The gate was very busy, and I decided to take a break, drink a coffee, and take it easy. I was distracted by a family who were hugging their relatives and crying. I didn't like it when my family dropped me off at the airport.

I would get that kind of feeling between wonder, sadness, and anxiety. But this time was very different. This time, I felt excited. I intended to complete an English course in the UK, so I planned to go to London, complete the course, and return to Sicily after a few months. But this time, I wasn't looking for revenge or looking to escape a situation: this time, I was in search of dreams, happiness, and achievements.

I already missed home as soon as I landed, but the feeling of learning something new made me happy.

* * *

One month later, I finished the last day of my English course. The next day would be my final exam, and I would earn the certificate.

I was getting ready to go back, but things went in a different way than I expected.

The 20th of March, 2017 was a cold Monday. I had just finished an interview with the front office manager of the Holiday Inn. A few hours later, the same manager sent me an offer letter: my interview was successful, and the job was mine if I wanted it. I was scared to start a new life here, but this was what I wanted.

I walked down Kensington High Street, watching the posh people walk into and out of shops. The houses were surrounded by tall trees, and the walls were so peculiar: I would say the most beautiful brick house exteriors in the London area.

What I like about walking in Kensington is that feeling of safety. People were happy and wealthy: most of them looked like they had just came out from a hairdresser, perfect in every single shape. Most of the women wore blonde, Californian balayage hair styles, a hat, beige coat, jeans, and white trainers while out walking with their dog, holding a latte from Costa and smiling at you with their bright teeth.

I kept walking until I reached my destination. It was a weird pub, called Churchill Arms, which was famed for the ornate display of flowers that covered the outside of the building. I was impressed.

I met one of my fellow students there, Michele. He was a nice guy, very smart: we were studying our IELTS together at the Kaplan college in Leicester Square. He was from the same city as me, and knew of most of my life experience.

When he told me he was looking for a job in London to stay and settle down in the city, I felt quite happy for him. I was thinking of starting a new life as well, so we had a beer and decided to eat some Thai food afterwards and talk about it.

I could not keep the good news to myself. He congratulated me, then asked, "Lexi, did you buy your ticket to go back?"

"Michele, I have to tell you the truth. I didn't buy the ticket yet, and I don't intend to buy one in the near future. I don't think I can see myself back in Sicily. That place has no future for an ambitious girl like me. With that interview today, the manager offered me a role as a receptionist with a good starting wage, so I don't know, to be honest."

"Alexa, are you crazy? What are you going to do with your job? Your car? Your flat? What about your boyfriend?"

"Well, I don't know," I answered, "I just want to have a life. I was always looking after my family: I didn't chase my dreams, I didn't have enough time to think about myself and what I wanted in my life. I think from now on, I have to prioritize my needs. It is about my happiness, and that is important to me, so they have to come first. I don't feel like staying in Sicily anymore. Sicily is my land, of course; all my memories are there, but I need to move on at some point.

My past was very difficult in Sicily, and although I had a job with the police and a nice boyfriend, I still felt unhappy; it's like something was always missing."

My dad had been released from the Mafia. Giuseppe would be in prison for life. The situation wasn't that bad: I could forget the past, get married, have a family, and still live comfortably, but that was far away from my mind.

"What about you, Michele? Did you apply for that job?"

"You know, Alexa, I will go be going back to Italy next week. I was thinking to stay—yes of course, London isn't Sicily—but I never thought about the expenses here; some students say that apparently a room to share is about six hundred pounds monthly, on top of the transport. And with our English, I don't think would be possible to get a good enough income at the beginning."

"Well, Michele, I think you need to do what you want; it's important that you are happy!"

"Sure, Alexa. Good luck with your English, and I will definitely send you a postcard from Sicily!"

* * *

A week later, I had called my family and informed them that I'd found a job in London.

Yes, after that news they were shocked. Chiara moved all my stuff out from the flat that I had shared with my mom. While I was looking for a place to stay in London, I called my commanding officer with the police in Sicily to let them know about my absence and sold my car online, my lovely black Alfa Romeo MiTo.

Although everyone was disappointed in my crazy choice, that choice was mine to make, and that day was a relief to me. The end of all that. The beginning of a new life, with freedom and liberation.

Finally, I could look at the sky and smile, thinking about that "gangster life," that corrupt life, that life with no job opportunities, and no goals. After so much fighting had ended, the unhappy feelings inside me had stopped forever; a new chapter of my life was just beginning. I was a newborn.

But as we say in Italy, "the whole world is a town."

And London demonstrated that very well to me.

Vanessa Nocera

Vanessa Nocera is thirty years old, a determined lady who sets many different goals in her life. She grew up on the island of Sicily, Italy. Vanessa is working towards a Master's Degree in business. She is also an event planner, promoting events, organizing conferences, and reaching excellent targets. She raises funds to support charity as a marathon runner. After over four years of military experience in the Italian Airforce and NATO, her ambitions will always ensure that she is successful in all her future undertakings. She loves travelling, learning new things, socialising, and sharing her new projects with the workforce. Vanessa lives in the United Kingdom.

Acknowledgments

Thanks to my editor, Ludovico Leone, who heard the idea for this book and decided to help me with the editing and publishing process. Thank you to my friend Stewart, who reviewed every single draft with me, encouraging me to dig deeper. Thanks to my furlough period during Covid-19, as this helped give me enough time to complete my writing. Thanks to my Mum, as during the Lockdown she pushed me to writing. And a big thank-you goes to you, my readers, for cheering and sharing my book.

Printed in Great Britain
by Amazon

27394141R00061